D1006161

Other Books by Witold Rybczynski

Paper Heroes

Taming the Tiger

Home

The Most Beautiful House in the World

Waiting for the Weekend

Looking Around

A Place for Art

City Life

A Clearing in the Distance

One Good Turn

The Look of Architecture

The Perfect House

Vizcaya (with Laurie Olin)

Last Harvest

My Two Polish Grandfathers

And Other Essays on the Imaginative Life

Witold Rybczynski

SCRIBNER

New York London Toronto Sydney

SCRIBNER
A Division of Simon & Schuster, Inc.
1230 Avenue of the Americas
New York, NY 10020

First Scribner hardcover edition February 2009

DESIGNED BY ERICH HOBBING

Text set in Stempel Garamond

Manufactured in the United States of America

1 3 5 7 9 10 8 6 4 2

Library of Congress Control Number: 2008030706

ISBN-13: 978-0-7432-3598-3
ISBN-10: 0-7432-3598-3

To the memory of
Mieczysław Hofman
(1881–1944)
and
Witold Rybczyński
(1881–1949)

CONTENTS

This action on the part of the mind practically amounts to a reaching out for the reasons of its interest, as only by its ascertaining them can the interest grow more various. This is the very education of our imaginative life.

—HENRY JAMES

My Two Polish Grandfathers

PREFACE

"Only when one has lost all curiosity about the future has one reached the age to write an autobiography" is how Evelyn Waugh began his own. Well, I still have some curiosity left, so this collection of essays, though autobiographical, is not quite a memoir. But part of my curiosity *is* about the past—my past. "Where are you from?" strangers at cocktail parties ask, innocently making friendly conversation. I'm never sure how to answer, for I'm an immigrant three times over. At age two, I was brought to England; when I was ten, I accompanied my family across the Atlantic to Canada; fifteen years ago—this time it was my own decision—I drove across the border to settle in the United States.

The move that probably influenced my life the most occurred before I was born—my parents' forced departure from Poland in 1939–40. The history of twentieth-century Europe has been roiled by many mass migrations impelled by economic disasters, religious persecution, redrawn national frontiers, and war. The displacement of people like my parents was hardly unique, but the peregrinations of

Poles during the Second World War, and their subsequent fate, are unusual and bear retelling.

Thus my first theme is movement, my parents', and then my own. England, Canada, Paris, Greece, Spain, Mexico, Nigeria, India—so much travel. It comes as a surprise, as I write today, for I do not think of myself as a nomad. Not for me the exotic vacation, the cultural junket; I like nothing better than staying put. But in hindsight I can see that my childhood moves fostered an unsentimental attitude to places. Experiencing different locales also developed a heightened awareness of my physical surroundings, and a more catholic taste, like being exposed early to different languages, or different foods. Not a bad thing.

Lack of roots produced something else—the slow emergence of an inner existence, the "education of an imaginative life." In my case, imagination was stimulated first by music, then by reading, and last by architecture. Architecture or, rather, the making of an architect, is my second theme. Some of these essays deal with the discovery of architecture—by a young student, by a fledgling practitioner, somewhat circuitously by an idealistic experimenter, and finally—definitively—by a wayward owner-builder. Architecture is so immobile, it might appear an odd preoccupation for someone with my background. But perhaps not. Building is always about creating a sense of place and permanence, both—for me—exotic sensations.

"For we possess nothing certainly except the past," says the narrator—an architectural painter—of *Brideshead Revisited,* Waugh's masterpiece about place and memory. He is right. But to possess the past, one has first to understand it, and understanding, as well as curiosity, is the chief motive for these essays.

Part I

My grandfather, Mieczysław Hofman (right), with his best friend, Jerzy Komorowski, outside Warsaw in the spring of 1939. An odd couple: the banker, more compact and controlled, not aloof, exactly, but with something held in reserve; and the industrialist, relaxed, expansive, apparently uninhibited.

The House Under Calton Hill

One year old, with my parents in Leven, Scotland, on April 10, 1944. I should have been a true Pole rather than a make-believe Scot.

I was born in the gray northern city of Edinburgh. I have no childhood memories of the place, no distant relatives, no family ties; the characteristic accent of its inhabitants is as foreign to my ears as Australian or Afrikaans. The Scottish capital was once called the Athens of the North, thanks to its intellectual traditions and to Calton Hill, an Acropolis-like promontory at its center. Most visitors remember the limestone architecture of the Royal Mile, the orderly Georgian crescents in New Town, and the cozy pubs on Princes Street. But that is not the native city of my imagination. A tinted lithograph of Edinburgh hung in my parents' bedroom. The artist, Samuel Dukinfield Swarbreck, was a nineteenth-century London lithographer of whom little is known, except that, in 1837, he made a tour of Scotland that resulted in a popular book of architectural views of Edinburgh, from which this print was culled. The lithograph shows the Jail Governor's House, newly built when Swarbreck saw the city, a battlemented fortress standing dramatically on the height of Calton Hill. At the foot of the hill is a rubble-strewn back street, with the corner of a Gothic church—Trinity College Church—across from a row of rough-looking houses with rugged slate roofs and tilting chimney pots. A workman mixes cement at the side of the street while his cart horse waits patiently, nose in feed bag. The atmosphere is quiet, the weather nondescript, not quite summer but not yet winter—September, according to Swarbreck's inscription. I looked at that picture often when I was a boy. Where was I born? There, I used to tell myself, that house on the left with the open third-floor window and the flowerpots on the sill. The house under Calton Hill.*

*The houses under Calton Hill, as well as Trinity College Church, were demolished in 1848 to make way for Edinburgh's central railway station.

I had a favorite childhood book, *The Scottish Tartans*. I remember spending many hours thumbing the pages of the postcard-size lexicon with its cloth cover and colored illustrations of kilted Scotsmen, hunting, fishing, and tossing the caber. I think I believed that, if I combed through it often enough, somewhere between the Robertsons and the Sinclairs, I would come across the crest, motto, and tartan of the Clan Rybczyński. My Scottishness was not entirely imagined, for I had an affidavit, a homemade certificate illustrated with a pretty watercolor drawing of an infant—me—in a cradle held between a crowned Polish eagle and a rampant Scottish lion. The typed text below read:

> WHEREAS, the parents of the boy,—Witold Rybczyński and his wife Anna,—being of Polish nationality, yet the land of birth of the child being Scotland, we, the undersigned, being ourselves true Scots do hereby willingly and without persuasion confer on the above-mentioned child immunity
>
> Frae Ghosties an' Ghoulies
> An' lang-leggity Beasties,
> Witches, Warlocks an' Wurricoes
> An' evil Spirits, an' a' Things
> Than gang Bump I' the Nicht.

I didn't know what a wurricoe was, but it sounded

fearsome.* The document was dated March 1943 and signed by members of the Stewart family, who were friends of my parents, including baby Kay, who boldly scrawled her name in childish capitals.

I appreciated the protective sentiment, but the two heraldic emblems only underscored my dilemma. All births have an accidental quality—why here and not there? why to these people and not those?—but mine was more accidental than most. I should have been born a thousand miles away, in Warsaw, not Edinburgh. I should have been a true Pole rather than a make-believe Scot.

My parents were married in Warsaw, in October 1937. My father, Witold, a twenty-nine-year-old electrical engineer, was from the southern province of Galicia. Poland, like most European countries, had several large cities but only one *metropole*—Warsaw—which was the nation's political, economic, and cultural capital. My father had been sent to the city to attend high school, and later university. After graduation, he worked in a Warsaw power cable factory owned by Škoda, a Czech conglomerate. The only child of divorced parents, he had had a peripatetic childhood, growing up on a succession of army posts with his mother and stepfather, Adam

*A wurricoe, according to a dictionary of Scottish terms, is a hobgoblin, although the origin of this ancient prayer is actually Cornish.

Korytowski, a career cavalry officer. Summers were spent in a southern country town with his father, a schoolteacher. My parents met in Warsaw. My mother, Anna, seven years younger, was in her final year of law school. Although she limped slightly as a result of childhood polio, she was attractive and socially active—my father was her third suitor. Her father was the president of a bank, and the family lived in a grand house in a fashionable district in the center of the city. While he was wealthy, he was not, by all accounts, a snob, and he approved the marriage. In lieu of a dowry, he provided a monthly allowance of five hundred zlotys, a generous sum, almost as much as my father's salary. He also arranged a better job for his new son-in-law with Lilpop, Rau & Loewenstein, a large industrial firm in Warsaw.

The newly married couple honeymooned in Italy. That country was in an unusual state of excitement; Mussolini and Hitler, the two strongmen of Europe, had just signed a formal pact against the Soviet Union. Despite its earlier defeat, Germany was a force again. The National Socialists had rebuilt the war-shattered economy, introduced conscription, and, contrary to the Versailles Treaty, created a formidable air force. Hitler had already flexed his muscles by remilitarizing the Rhineland. The political situation seemed to have had little effect on my parents, however, who spent a happy month in Venice, Florence, Rome, and Naples.

The following spring, the Wehrmacht marched into Austria. Six months later, Hitler proclaimed the Sudetenland a German protectorate, Chamberlain and Daladier capitulated at Munich, and Poland and Hungary ignominiously took advantage of the confusion to annex parts of Czechoslovakia. While these portentous events were taking place, my parents were on a kayaking trip in the foothills of the Beskidy Mountains. Movies and novels sometimes archly portray people leading normal lives and even enjoying themselves while disaster lurks around the corner—what fools they must have been not to perceive their fates, we think. This has always seemed to me a facile view. People living in 1938—or in 1913, for that matter—may have sensed war over the horizon, but they could hardly foresee the enormity of what was to come.

In fact, my parents were all too mindful of their country's precarious political situation. The republic of Poland was barely twenty years old, younger than they. In the 1770s, after years of political instability and near anarchy, the weakened Polish kingdom had been partitioned by its neighbors: the western portion taken by Prussia, the eastern part by the Russian Empire, and the southern part by the Austro-Hungarian Empire. Thus, my father had been born a subject of the emperor Franz Joseph I, and my mother, of Czar Nicholas II.

The new republic of Poland came into being in

November 1918, following the collapse of the occupying powers in the confused aftermath of the First World War and the Russian Revolution. (The Bolsheviks immediately attacked the new state, and were resoundingly defeated.) With such a history, the Poles trusted neither of their two largest neighbors. Instead they relied on treaties with the distant French and British, though only half-believing that these would be honored. Polish history had yielded a national character that was patriotic, stubborn, and often skeptical if not downright pessimistic. "Poland isn't yet lost, as long as we are living," begins the national anthem, although the doleful words are set to a gay mazurka.

My parents intended to start a family just as soon as my mother, who had completed her law studies, passed the bar exam—a year or two at the most. They were financially well-off since my mother's father also provided them with a rent-free apartment in one of the buildings he owned. My mother's parents were anxious to see a grandchild—their first. So, I was just around the corner. At least, that was the plan.

In July 1939, as the political tensions in Europe heightened, the Polish armed forces began to mobilize. Since Lilpop manufactured railway rolling stock and trucks, my father was exempt from military service. On September 1, using a staged incident as a pretext, Germany invaded Poland. The Luftwaffe disabled the small Polish air force on the ground and immediately began bombing Warsaw and other cities. Four days later, my father's factory was ordered to relocate to a plant about fifty miles south of the capital. Bidding a hasty farewell to my mother, he set out with a convoy of vehicles. He took overnight things, because he expected to be away for only a few days. It would be thirty years before he returned to Warsaw.

The story of Polish cavalry vaingloriously charging Panzers is apocryphal—or German propaganda—but it accurately reflects the imbalance between the forces. The Poles were outnumbered—they had about 40 divisions against the attackers' 60—and badly outgunned: only 150 tanks against 2,600; a mere 400 warplanes against 2,000. The unevenness of the conflict is reflected in the final casualty count: about 60,000 Polish servicemen (and many more civilians) killed versus less than 14,000 fatal Wehrmacht casualties. It was not only a question of firepower. The blitzkrieg, or lightning war, surged into Poland from three directions: Germany, East Prussia, and Czechoslovakia. The flat Polish plain—the country's name is derived from *pole,* which means "fields"—offered few obstructions to the invading forces, not even swollen rivers or muddy roads, for that autumn was sunny and dry.

Poland's treaty with France and Great Britain stipulated that, in the case of a German attack,

Poland would resist for two weeks, to give its allies time to mobilize and mount a major offensive across the Rhine. This would oblige Germany to divide its forces between two fronts, and since the Allies outnumbered the German forces in the west, a successful outcome seemed inevitable. Although France and Britain declared war within three days of the invasion, two weeks came and went and no offensive took place. Planes of the Royal Air Force did make a few flights over Poland, but they dropped only leaflets. In the history of the Second World War, the invasion of Poland has become little more than a footnote, but the story of French and British perfidy was a big part of my childhood upbringing.

Keeping just ahead of the rapidly advancing Germans, my father's convoy passed its original destination and drove into Galicia, in the southeastern corner of Poland. There the party divided, some continuing south, and a group of volunteers, including my father, going east to link up with Polish army units near the Russian border. They were surprised to find villages flying red flags. The Russians were coming. That very day—September 17—Stalin, who a week earlier had made a secret alliance with Hitler, ordered his army to invade Poland. Boxed in, my father's ill-fated convoy turned back and crossed into Romania, with which Poland had a nonaggression treaty.

Despite the treaty, my father's group promptly

found itself in an internment camp. The small town of Fălticeni was crowded with Polish refugees, government officials, and military personnel. The retreat was a national humiliation, yet the Poles had no reason to be ashamed—they had resisted Germany for a month, longer than the mighty French army would manage the following year. But surrender was inevitable. Despite their reputation for romantic gestures, the Poles had no intention of fighting to the last man. Between them, the Germans and the Russians took a million prisoners. The Polish government and most of the general staff were interned by Romania. Yet immediately, a provisional government was established in Paris under a new prime minister and commander in chief, General Władysław Sikorski. Sikorski, who was an opponent of the authoritarian Piłsudski regime, which had taken power in a 1926 military coup and had been living in self-imposed exile in Paris, was a renowned military leader who had commanded the forces that defeated the Russians in the 1919–20 war. French and British radio broadcast his appeal for all Poles who could to join the reconstituted Polish army in France.

The expatriate call to arms did not strike Poles as unusual. There was a long tradition, established during the century of partition, of émigrés fighting under foreign flags. Polish patriots such as Kościuszko and Pułaski took part in the American War of Independence, and there were Polish regiments in Bonaparte's army in Italy. Almost a hundred thousand Poles followed the emperor on his ill-fated winter march to Moscow, and Polish lancers fought the British at Waterloo. After Russia put down a popular uprising in Poland in 1830, Polish regiments appeared in Hungary, Italy, and France, often fighting their old enemy, the Austrians. During the First World War, thousands of Poles fought (sometimes each other) in so-called Polish legions under German, Russian, and Austrian commands. Hence, for a nation that had lacked a state, let alone a standing army, for more than a century, Poland had a long martial tradition.

My father, who had spent a compulsory year in the military after graduating from university, decided with three colleagues to try to get to Paris. One of the men had a Ford, and they also had a large Buick that belonged to Lilpop, which assembled cars for General Motors. Leaving the improvised internment camp was not a problem, but they needed exit permits to cross the border, as well as transit visas for Yugoslavia and Italy. They concocted a scheme: they claimed that the Buick belonged to General Sikorski, and that they were delivering it to him in Paris. The far-fetched ploy worked, and they managed to get the required papers. The two cars set out, trunks and backseats dangerously loaded with containers of gasoline, for gas was cheaper in Romania than in Yugoslavia and Italy.

One day out of Bucharest, the oldest member of the group fell ill, and since they were afraid to go to the local hospital, they holed up in a hotel for three days until he recovered. Then they continued west into Yugoslavia. In Belgrade they were to pick up French visas, but these weren't ready and they had to wait. This time they didn't stay in their hotel but went sightseeing. After driving through the Croatian mountains, they crossed the Italian border near Trieste. Italy was officially neutral but distinctly pro-German. Padua was a bittersweet experience for my father, who had been there on his honeymoon two years earlier. He found time to stop at the Basilica di Sant'Antonio and offer a prayer to the patron saint of lost persons for a swift reunion with his wife.* Eventually, they ran low on gas. The Italian service stations were manned by black-shirted Fascists who looked intimidating but cheerfully provided ration coupons and waved them to the front of the line. The journey continued uneventfully to the French border, along the Riviera as far as Marseilles, and then north to Paris. They dutifully delivered the Buick to the headquarters of the Polish command—by then the fiction had become a reality—which

*Many years later, my parents gratefully named my younger brother Anthony.

was in the Hôtel Regina on the rue de Rivoli, across from the Louvre. At the hotel my father ran into his mother, who was there with his stepfather, now a general.

The journey sounds more like Jerome K. Jerome—Three Men in a Buick—than John Buchan; still, it couldn't have been a picnic. Looking at the long, looping route penciled on my map, I can only marvel at the brave seventeen-day, eighteen-hundred-mile drive across a Europe nervous and primed for war.

Paris was awash in Poles who had responded to Sikorski's appeal. It is estimated that the Polish army in France in 1939–40 numbered a hundred thousand men. Half were escapees like my father, the rest were local volunteers, chiefly Polish coal miners from the region around Lille, many of whom had fought on the Republican side in the Spanish Civil War. Sikorski had a grand plan to conscript Polish emigrants from Canada and the United States, but this unrealistic scheme came to naught. His military force included a destroyer flotilla and two submarines that had left port ahead of the Germans (and sailed to England), as well as several thousand experienced (though planeless) pilots. Not all escaping Poles made it to France—my father had been lucky. Romania, yielding to Germany's pressure (the following year the country would formally join the Axis), closed its borders. Several thousand Polish soldiers escaped to Bulgaria and Turkey, ending up in French Syria and eventually joining the British army in Palestine.

My father enlisted at the Bessières army barracks near Clichy and was commissioned a second lieutenant, given a World War I–vintage French uniform, and told to report to Versailles for signals training. He spoke some French, having spent two summers working in Parisian power stations as a university intern. It was an odd experience, to be in peacetime France after war-torn Poland. This was the period that the French called *la drôle de guerre,* the phony war. Hitler had invaded Norway and Denmark, but nothing was happening on the Western Front, where the two opposing armies faced each other, from the Maginot Line to the English Channel.

Meanwhile, my mother was in Warsaw. She had survived the three-week siege of the city, which left tens of thousands of dead and wounded, and widespread destruction from bombs and artillery. Although neither her apartment nor her parents' house was seriously damaged, living conditions were difficult in the occupied city, with curfews, food shortages, and no news of the outside world since the Germans had confiscated all radios. Many of her friends had been killed, and her husband's closest relative, his cousin Marian, was in a prisoner-of-war camp in Germany. The city was crowded with refugees from western Poland, which was now part of the Reich. Eastern Poland had been annexed by the Soviet Union; the area in between, including Warsaw, was a German administrative district, named—unaccountably in fractured French—the General Gouvernement. The state of Poland had once more ceased to exist.

My mother spent afternoons working in a hospital and mornings teaching her nine-year-old brother and other children in an improvised schoolroom (the Germans having closed all the schools). She had no idea what had happened to her husband. His employers thought that he might have escaped to Romania, but they weren't sure. He sent several postcards from Italy during his journey, addressed to different friends in Warsaw since he didn't want to compromise my mother with the German authorities. Eventually, one of these cards reached my mother, and after a two-and-a-half-month silence she learned that he was alive. While there was no postal service between occupied Poland and France, she was able to respond via an intermediary in Italy.

At the beginning of 1940, my mother decided that she would try to join her husband in Paris. Her father objected; after all, the war would surely soon be over, he said, and they would be reunited. Her friends, by contrast, encouraged her to leave. She managed to get a passport and, after a long wait, secured an exit visa for still-neutral Italy, pleading ill health and the need for a warmer climate—her polio infirmity suddenly an asset. From his end, my father arranged a French visa. She left at the beginning of April, two days after Hitler's occupation of Denmark and Norway, taking a train via Vienna to Milan. By then the French visa had expired, and she found herself stranded, waiting for new travel papers. Milan was hardly hospitable. Fascism had originated in northern Italy, and, as Mussolini and Hitler grew closer, the atmosphere in the city became increasingly hostile to foreigners.

In the spring my father was posted to Camp Coëtquidan in Brittany, which served as the staging point for the Polish forces in France, many of whom had no previous military training. Coëtquidan was a far cry from Versailles. The Napoleonic-era artillery base had last been used during the First World War by the American Expeditionary Force. Captain Harry S. Truman had trained an artillery battery there; my father, a mere second lieutenant, was in charge of a signals platoon. Conditions in the camp were dismal: old wooden barracks with broken windows and primitive heating. The men trained in moth-eaten uniforms with rifles that had last seen service in the Franco-Prussian War. The haughty French instructors did not bother to disguise their disdain for the defeated Poles.

In early May, Germany launched a broad offensive through Holland, Belgium, and Luxembourg.

Days later, seven Panzer divisions unexpectedly emerged from the Ardennes forest, crossing the Meuse River and pushing through the French lines. On May 20, an armored spearhead reached the channel, cutting the Allied armies in two and isolating the British Expeditionary Force with its back to the sea. Catastrophe loomed.

That same fateful day, in front of Camp Coëtquidan's main gate, my parents were reunited. They hadn't seen each other for eight months. They spent that night in the local railroad station hotel, then moved in with my father's mother and his stepfather, who was camp commandant. They lived in the Château du Tertre, a commandeered country house a few miles from the camp. My father bicycled daily to his barracks. It would have been idyllic but for the rapidly deteriorating situation at the front.

By the beginning of June, the once-distant war was closing in on Brittany. The British had successfully evacuated the encircled part of their force from the beaches of Dunkirk, and the Germans were steadily pushing back the demoralized and crumbling French army. On June 14 the Wehrmacht entered Paris, and four days later German advance units arrived in the city of Rennes, only twenty miles from Coëtquidan. The situation in the camp was uncertain. Two Polish divisions had been sent to reinforce the French Second Army in the Vosges, and the remaining soldiers, only partly trained and poorly armed, could offer little resistance. What was left of the British Expeditionary Force—some 136,000 men—was about to be evacuated from Cherbourg, Brest, and Saint-Nazaire. Speaking from London over the BBC, Sikorski, who had been assured by Winston Churchill that the British would continue to fight, once more issued a general order: his men in France should make their way as best they could to western ports, where ships would take them to Britain.

The camp was evacuated in what can best be described as an organized rout. My father found himself fleeing once more, and once more apart from my mother, for she was transported separately with other dependents. His military convoy headed for Saint-Nazaire, the closest port, but all ships had left. La Rochelle, too, was empty. They passed the smoldering hulks of bombed freighters in the Gironde estuary. Continuing south, they reached Bordeaux just ahead of the German forces. By then, Marshal Pétain, who was now head of state, had announced that he would seek an armistice, and on June 22, little more than five weeks after the commencement of hostilities, France formally surrendered.

Crossing the flat plain south of Bordeaux, my father's group made slow progress on roads crowded with fleeing civilians and lines of army trucks. Passing the resort city of Biarritz, they finally arrived at Saint-Jean-de-Luz, only a few miles from the Spanish border. The port was the chief embarkation point for the Polish troops, who set up a defensive perimeter around the town, as much against the French (who, having made their own peace, were not sympathetic to the fleeing Poles) as against the swiftly advancing Germans. It was unclear whether safety lay in sailing to Britain, and risking attack by German planes and U-boats, or in crossing to Spain, which was officially neutral but whose dictator, Franco, was sympathetic to the Germans.

The town was packed with soldiers, including remnants of the British army. Confusion reigned. In the midst of the turmoil, my father and mother were once again reunited. They decided to try to board one of the cargo ships that was anchored offshore, but this proved difficult. My mother, who spoke English, met a contingent of British soldiers who offered her passage but would not take my father, since technically he belonged to the French army, now hors de combat. Then a place became available with the Polish troops, but not for my mother since she was a civilian. My parents declined both offers and decided to stay together.

The pair spent a harrowing twenty-four hours in Saint-Jean-de-Luz, sleeping in a car in the town square, which was crowded with thousands of soldiers. My father might have approached his stepfather and mother, who were also there, and obtained passage with the high-ranking officers, but a stubborn sense of propriety prevented him from trading on his family connection. Then he met a friend from the camp who had driven his own car from Brittany, accompanied by his girlfriend. The enterprising Lieutenant Orlowski found a local fisherman who would row them to the ships for a few thousand francs. The two couples boarded a Dutch collier, the *Baron Nairn,* whose decks were already crowded with soldiers.

It's difficult for me to reconcile my childhood image of my parents—circumspect, cautious, to my immature eyes unadventurous—with these audacious individuals, crisscrossing Europe, setting out into the unknown at a moment's notice, and persevering in the face of one calamity after another. At my father's age I was leading the settled existence of an assistant professor, braving nothing more hazardous than departmental faculty meetings. I wonder if I would have found the inner resources to deal with a life turned upside down, as he had done.

The *Baron Nairn* sailed at once. The threat of attack by the Luftwaffe hung in the air, but no enemy planes were sighted, and in three days the ship berthed safely in Plymouth. My father and the other soldiers boarded a train bound for Glasgow, and my mother was sent to an aliens' transit camp in London. Only eighteen thousand Poles managed to escape from France, not only from Saint-Jean-de-Luz but also from Bordeaux and smaller ports in

Brittany. (The rest of the Polish army was scattered to the four winds: those who had come from the Lille coal mines simply went home and became Frenchmen once more; one Polish division escaped to Switzerland, where it was interned for the rest of the war; a large number of soldiers went underground and formed a separate organization within the French resistance.)

Except for several thousand pilots, who were attached to the Royal Air Force and immediately thrown into the Battle of Britain, and the naval personnel, who stayed with their vessels, the evacuated Polish troops were sent to Scotland. Their stated military purpose, while training and regrouping, was to man concrete bunkers and pillboxes on the Fife peninsula, in the unlikely event that the Germans should launch an invasion from occupied Norway, 350 miles across the North Sea. In truth, the British, who had lost most of their military equipment at Dunkirk, were hard put to make immediate use of the Poles.

The fall of France had a strong effect on the Polish servicemen, who believed the French army to be invincible. Poles were generally Francophiles, not only because of historic sympathies but also because France had always been a safe haven for Polish exiles; Chopin and Madame Curie were equally celebrated in Warsaw and Paris. But England was an unknown, Scotland even more so. One can only imagine what the Scots thought of the foreigners with unpronounceable names who had suddenly appeared in their midst.

For the second time the Poles went about rebuilding their army. My father was assigned to the signals unit of a tank battalion, then several months later temporarily seconded to one of the cadre brigades, so named because they consisted largely of officers, there being insufficient enlisted men. His commander was Colonel Stanisław Sosabowski, a veteran soldier who was preparing for clandestine action in occupied Poland and needed radio operators. My father's introduction to the brigade was a monthlong course at Inverlochy Castle, in the Western Highlands, in marksmanship, mine laying, and other sabotage techniques.

By then, my mother, who had been released from the aliens' camp, was also in Scotland. Her first job was with one of the many Polish newspapers that had sprung up to inform the servicemen, few of whom spoke English, about the progress of the war. Later she worked as an orderly in a military hospital near Perth. She and my father saw each other whenever he managed to get leave.

"One can see them in the evening, or on Sundays eating fish and chips in small Scottish towns, or walking with their girl friends," reads a contemporary description of the Poles in Scotland. "They organize their own amateur shows and their own libraries, and they publish an amazing number of newspapers and books." My father now had family obligations, not only to his wife but also to his mother. She was living with her husband, the general, on the Isle of Bute, west of Glasgow. There were a couple of hundred Polish staff officers on Bute. The isolated holiday resort has been described as the place where "Sikorski banished his political opponents." Whether it was politics—Poles were chronic schemers—or simply that the disorganized withdrawal from Camp Coëtquidan had required a scapegoat, Adam Korytowski was under virtual house arrest. The poor man died within a year.

In September 1941, my father's cadre unit was reconstituted as the First Independent Parachute Brigade. It was "independent" because, unlike the other Polish units, it was not under British command but reported directly to the exiled Polish government in London. Parachutists had been used for the first time with great success by the Germans in their invasion of Holland and Belgium. The Poles intended to deploy the brigade—which eventually numbered twenty-five hundred men—to liberate their homeland. Sosabowski was a hard-driving commander. Airborne forces in most armies were composed of volunteers; not so the brigade. My father's transfer papers back to the tank battalion simply disappeared. The training was rigorous, since paratroopers, like commandos, were expected to form self-sufficient fighting units and be skilled in a variety of combat situations. My father later often joked about his career as a parachutist, but, at thirty-three, he was old to be jumping out of planes. He practiced controlled falls from a hundred-foot tower and made his first live jump—at a thousand feet—at the British army's parachute training base near Manchester. On his second sortie, this time from five hundred feet, he encountered turbulence, landed hard, and broke his left arm.* After several months of convalescence—made easier by the fact that he was in the hospital where my mother worked—he returned to the brigade. There was more training and signals work, though not, for the moment, more jumping. During this period he was posted to London for a month, preparing an inventory of the electrical power grid in eastern Pomerania, then a part of Germany. It was January 1942, German U-boats were taking a terrible toll on Allied shipping in the Atlantic, Hitler had already launched his ill-starred offensive against the Soviet Union, and although the United States had just entered the war and Britain no longer stood alone, the outcome was far from clear—yet the Poles were already planning postwar reparations!

When my father returned from London, his

*A later casualty of the Manchester course was the forty-year-old Evelyn Waugh, who spent his six-month convalescence writing *Brideshead Revisited.*

brigade was stationed in Leven, across the broad Firth of Forth from Edinburgh. My mother, who had left the hospital and enlisted in the army, was now an education officer in a light artillery unit in St. Andrews, about ten miles farther up the coast. This was close enough for my father to bicycle there on weekends. I was conceived that summer. My pregnant mother resigned her commission and found a room in Leven. I was born early the following year in the recently renamed Ignacy Paderewski Wing of Edinburgh's General Western Hospital, delivered by a Polish army doctor and a Scottish nurse.

A combination of bad and good luck, large and small accidents—and determination—brought my parents together in this place at this particular time. At any point, the strands of the story might have broken, or been woven into a different pattern. If Hitler had postponed his invasion of France in 1940, I might have been born in Brittany. If my parents had not been able to get on a ship in Saint-Jean-de-Luz and had escaped to Spain, my birthplace might have been Bilbao. On the other hand, if my father had been captured by the Germans or the Russians, or interned in Romania, or if my mother had been unable to leave Poland or gotten permanently stuck in Milan, I might not have been born at all. Is it any surprise that I am by nature a fatalist? Or perhaps that's just my skeptical Polish genes.

Wartime

London, 1947. I'm sitting on what looks like church steps with Colonel Jerzy Emisarski, a family friend. By World War II's end, almost a quarter of a million Poles were in uniform, and more than half of them chose to stay in Britain.

I watched many war movies as a boy, but the plots never had anything to do with my family's circumstances—nobody made films about driving Buicks across Europe, or about Poles training in Scotland. Much later, I did see *A Bridge Too Far,* which describes the massive Allied airborne operation, called Market Garden, in which the First Independent Parachute Brigade took part. In the movie, Gene Hackman plays Sosabowski, the brigade's commander, as a prickly outsider who is highly dubious about the plan. The aim of Market Garden, devised by General Montgomery, was to capture a series of bridges in Holland by dropping airborne troops far behind the German lines. It was an ill-conceived operation that turned into a disaster. In the movie, Sosabowski's skepticism is vindicated; in real life, his foresight did not endear him to the British, who had him relieved of his command. My father did not take part in Market Garden. In March 1944—just six months before the operation—he was ordered to report to the offices of the Polish high command in London, and was told that he was being detached from the parachute brigade to take part in a special operation in support of the underground resistance in Poland.

Five years into the war, the situation in Poland had reached a crucial juncture. The German invasion of Russia—since 1941 no longer part of the Axis—had foundered. After overwhelming Russian victories at Stalingrad and Kursk, and the Allies' decision to invade Europe through France rather than the Balkans, it appeared certain that Poland would be liberated not by Tommies or GIs but by the Ivans. In the eyes of the Polish government in London, it was critical that their country not simply fall into the lap of the Soviet Union. The Poles had every reason to distrust Stalin, who had earlier joined Hitler in the dismemberment of Poland. Yet despite Russia's treachery, Sikorski and Stalin signed a treaty that established diplomatic relations. Left unresolved was the status of Galicia (today part of Ukraine) and White Ruthenia (today Belarus)—which had been annexed by the Soviets following their 1939 invasion. Stalin claimed these lands as a historic part of Russia, while the Polish government demanded their return. Churchill proposed that Poland acknowledge Russia's claim and accept German lands in the west in exchange, but that alternative was unacceptable to Sikorski. The impasse deepened in 1943, when the Germans, who by then had advanced deep into Ukraine, announced that they had discovered a mass grave near Smolensk containing the remains of several thousand Polish officers. The fate of the fourteen thousand officers who had been captured by the Soviets in 1939 and had disappeared had long been a matter of conjecture. Now the answer was clear: they had been executed by the Russians. When Sikorski demanded an official investigation of the affair, Stalin angrily severed diplomatic relations with the Poles.*

*The truth of Sikorski's claim was finally confirmed in 1990, when Mikhail Gorbachev publicly admitted Russian culpability for the so-called Katyn massacre.

Neither the Allied governments nor the American press credited Sikorski's claim, and the increasingly isolated Polish leadership was accused of endangering the Grand Alliance. The Soviet Union was now a key partner in the war and had to be placated—the British and the Americans knew it, the Russians certainly knew it, only the Poles were out of step. "The root of the trouble for Poland," writes W. J. M. Mackenzie, a sympathetic British historian, was "that its pre-war governing class (which was strongly represented in exile) had the instincts and traditions of a Great Power—a Great Power of the seventeenth century and earlier, with few resources acquired since that time to justify its claim."

The Polish government in London devised a risky strategy to finesse any attempt by the Soviet Union to "liberate" Poland. They planned a national uprising, timed to break out just before the arrival of the Red Army, and spearheaded by the Armia Krajowa, or Home Army. Although this underground force numbered as many as 380,000, only about a tenth of its members were armed. Since 1941, the government in exile in London had been parachuting arms into Poland from a secret base near Cambridge, but this operation was severely constrained by the great distance, a thousand miles, the absolute limit of current aircraft. Eventually the base was relocated to Tunisia, and after the successful Allied invasion of

Sicily, it was moved to southern Italy. That was where my father was being sent.

Before his departure, he was sworn in to the Polish section of the Special Operations Executive, a British wartime secret service that infiltrated agents into occupied countries to carry out sabotage and subversion. The SOE, which Churchill once called the "ministry of ungentlemanly warfare," since it operated under the cover of the Ministry of Economic Warfare, was active in the Balkans, North Africa, and the Far East, but above all in occupied Europe. Each country had its own section. Thanks to Sikorski's close relationship with Churchill, the Polish SOE enjoyed a great deal of autonomy, operating its own radio communications and ciphers, and running its own agents, all under the direct control of the Polish government.

Since my father would no longer be in Scotland, my mother decided to move to London. She had visited England before the war, was fluent in English, and hoped to augment my father's small lieutenant's pay by working as a translator in one of the Polish government offices. The move was ill-timed. My mother and I arrived in London on May 2, 1944, and on June 13 the Germans launched their first V-1 attacks on the city. Soon the unmanned flying bombs, known as buzz bombs, were falling all over London, including the suburban neighborhood where we lived. We returned to Scotland. Together with her widowed mother-in-law, my mother rented rooms in Peebles, a pretty town in the hilly countryside south of Edinburgh.

By then my father was on the high seas, his departure from Clydeside having been delayed for a week by the Normandy invasion. He disembarked at Naples. The headquarters of the Polish SOE operation was near Brindisi, in the village of Latiano, on the heel of the Italian boot. The base, code-named Bazall, included a training school for agents, a unit that packed parachute containers, and a radio transmitting station, which was my father's responsibility. The radio operators were, like him, ex-paratroopers who, in a pinch, could be sent to Poland. Ten Polish aircrews were stationed in Brindisi, which is about six hundred miles from southern Poland. The half dozen airplanes included converted four-engine bombers—Liberators and Halifaxes—and small Dakota DC-3s that could land on clandestine airstrips to pick up people and documents. The flights carried radio operators, couriers, and agents, as well as containers filled with arms, explosives, and radio transmitters. One of these missions, which took place shortly after my father's arrival, concerned the V-2 rocket. While the V-1 was a pilotless aircraft, the V-2 was a true ballistic missile, more accurate and with a greater range. After the Peenemünde testing base was bombed (thanks to Polish

SOE intelligence), the Germans moved the rocket test site to Poland. When the Home Army got its hands on an unexploded V-2, an SOE plane from Italy picked up a courier with not only drawings of the missile but also parts of its guidance system.

The Latiano signals platoon was billeted in a large villa. There were periodic leaves in Brindisi and visits to a nearby First Aid Nursing Yeomanry base. The so-called FANYs were young English women volunteers who worked as drivers and nurses' aides and ran a safe house for Polish agents. Unknown to the Poles, FANYs also sometimes served as SOE operatives, and their job in Latiano was to keep an eye on the independent Poles. According to my father, the close observation produced at least three marriages.

The chief mission of the Latiano base was to support the planned Polish uprising. The operation to liberate Poland in the face of a Soviet advance was grandly named Operation Burza, or Storm. Since the lightly armed Home Army could hardly defeat the Wehrmacht on its own, a successful uprising demanded cooperation with the advancing Russians. The problem was that the exiled Polish government remained at loggerheads with the Soviet Union. A year earlier, General Sikorski had died in a suspicious plane accident that many Poles believed was the result of Soviet sabotage, but his successor did not enjoy Churchill's confidence, and lacked the stature to deal directly with Stalin. Moreover, the Polish political leadership quarreled among themselves, some seeing Russia as a treacherous but necessary ally, others as an outright enemy.

Operation Storm was set in motion in northern and southern Poland. The Russian response was to simply arrest the Polish officers and absorb the enlisted men into their own ranks. Seeing their original plan for a general uprising in the countryside stymied, the Home Army commanders changed tactics and decided to take and hold Warsaw. They reasoned that the international attention paid to an uprising in the capital would constrain Soviet behavior. On August 1, 1944, following reports that Red Army tanks had been seen in the suburbs of the city and that the Germans were retreating, the Warsaw uprising was set in motion. In fact, the intelligence was faulty; the Russian tanks were merely a small advance party—the main body of the Soviet army was still sixty miles away—and the Wehrmacht was far from routed. The Germans reacted swiftly, bringing up reinforcements to halt the Russian advance and dispatching units to Warsaw to put down the insurgency.

The prematurely called uprising became a full-fledged urban battle. The poorly armed Home Army, which in Warsaw numbered about forty-five thousand men and women (among them, my mother's younger sister, Krysia), found itself facing

Tiger tanks, heavy artillery, and Stuka dive-bombers. Worse was to come. The Home Army commanders had assumed that the uprising would be supported by the Polish armed forces, particularly the air force and the parachute brigade. But on August 1, the Allied armies were stuck in Normandy, the flying distance to Warsaw was still too great for fighter aircraft and only barely within range of supply flights, while the parachute brigade, independent in name only, had been appropriated by the British for Market Garden. Since the Home Army had not managed to capture the airport, an alternative would have been for aircraft to refuel at Russian air bases in eastern Poland. However, Stalin forbade Allied planes to land and refuel behind his lines, or even to fly over Russian-held territory. He had no reason to help the Home Army, since he backed a small Communist Polish resistance group—the Armia Ludowa, or People's Army—which did not recognize the government in London and was ready to cooperate with the Soviet Union.*

That left the SOE air base in Brindisi. The British sent four squadrons of planes from the Royal Air Force and the South African Air Force to supplement the Polish aircraft. The flight from Brindisi to Warsaw—a total distance of nine hundred miles—

*The People's Army, which never numbered more than ten thousand, was tiny compared with the Home Army.

was harrowing. The slow bombers, flying at night without fighter escorts, had to cross heavily defended Hungary and Czechoslovakia, and when they reached Warsaw they were greeted by antiaircraft fire and fighter planes. Of a total of 196 flights from Italy, only 42 managed to get through. But since the smoke-shrouded, burning city made accurate drops impossible, of the 42 drops, only 25 actually reached the resistance fighters. Out of 196, only 25 made it! The losses in planes were so severe that the British and the South Africans were ordered to stop flying. The Poles continued, but to little avail.

The disastrous uprising was a desperate gambit, but the people of Warsaw were at the end of their tether. The five years of German occupation had been a cruel and barbarous reign of terror, characterized by random arrests, executions, and deportations. This was an occupation unlike those of, say, Copenhagen or Amsterdam. The Nazis' long-term plan was to create a German state in Poland and to eradicate Polish culture. To that end, they targeted the clergy, teachers, intellectuals, and, of course, the Jews, who were about a quarter of the city's population. The last were forced to live in a walled ghetto. In 1943, as increasing numbers of Jews were being deported to death camps, the survivors in the Warsaw Ghetto staged an armed revolt. The revolt, which lasted three weeks, was cruelly put down, the remaining Jews either killed or sent to concentration camps.

The uprising of the Home Army did not fare much better. The commanders planned Operation Storm to last a week, only until the Red Army arrived; instead, the fighting went on for *nine* weeks. Finally, as the air drops dwindled to nothing, the desperate fighters simply ran out of ammunition. Those who could not escape were obliged to surrender. The human cost was appalling: in addition to twenty thousand military casualties, two hundred thousand civilians died, most executed by the Germans in reprisals, used as human shields, or indiscriminately shot. Moreover, the city itself was punished. What happened to Warsaw, while less widely known than the firebombing of Dresden, the destruction of Coventry, or the bombing of Hiroshima, ranks as the worst urban disaster of the Second World War. Hitler ordered a city whose prewar population had exceeded one and a quarter million people to be razed. After evacuating the remaining population, and systematically looting the city of municipal infrastructure, factory machinery, and personal belongings, the German army spent several months blowing up the surviving monuments and major public buildings.

My mother's family passed the entire uprising in their home. They had been turned out the previous year by the occupation authorities, who decreed the neighborhood *Nur für Deutsche* (for Germans only), but had moved back just before the uprising broke out. The central district in which their house was located held out until the end. After the cessation of hostilities, German trucks with loudspeakers ordered everyone to evacuate. Four months later, when the Germans finally left Warsaw—just before the Russians arrived—my mother's sister Wisia returned to the deserted city. Miraculously, although most of the buildings on their street had been destroyed, she found the house more or less intact. "I collected some papers, photographs lying about," she later recalled. "I squatted in a small caretaker's room at the back—the windows were blown out, there was no heating." It must have been eerie, an empty house in an empty city, the mounds of fresh graves visible under the snow, the rear garden having been turned into a burial ground.

The destruction of Warsaw was a bitter defeat for my father and the men of the SOE in Italy. Clandestine flights to southern Poland continued, but with the Polish government in London in disarray (both the prime minister and the commander in chief had resigned in the wake of the failed uprising), morale was low. One of the radio operators in Latiano broke down and committed suicide. In February 1945, with Poland almost entirely overrun by the Soviet Union, the Home Army was officially disbanded. Finally, in March, Bazall was closed down.

My father left Italy a month later. Having boarded a ship in Naples, he disembarked in Clydeside, near

Glasgow, arriving in London the following day. It was May 8, V-E Day. The streets were thronged with celebrating crowds. He joined thousands of people in Whitehall to hear Churchill speak. For the rejoicing British, it was victory, for my father, something considerably less.

It has been said that the Poles fought two wars in 1939–1945, one against Germany, which they won, and the other against the Soviet Union, which they lost. As Sikorski had anticipated, Soviet liberation foreshadowed Soviet domination. The Polish state was on the map, but it was independent in name only. Stalin installed a provisional government whose main role was to ensure that the forthcoming election would be won by a Soviet-backed workers' party, despite the fact that the majority of Poles were strongly anti-Communist. The English and the Americans complained, but they were not about to go to war over rigged elections. What was left of the Polish underground resistance refused to accept the new state of affairs, and civil war broke out in several parts of the country. The NKVD (the Soviet security police) arrested thousands of opponents of the increasingly totalitarian regime, especially ex-members of the Home Army, whose leadership languished in Russian prisons.

The size of the Polish army serving under British command had increased dramatically since 1940; by the war's end, there were almost a quarter of a million Poles in uniform. They included volunteers, liberated prisoners of war, and defecting Wehrmacht conscripts from western parts of Poland. The largest contingent consisted of Polish servicemen who had been captured by the Russians at the beginning of the war and imprisoned in Siberia. When Stalin changed sides in 1941, he agreed to release more than a hundred thousand of these prisoners, offering them a chance to join the Red Army. Not surprisingly, most refused, and, led by General Władysław Anders, they crossed the Kazakh desert and Persia on foot, ultimately arriving in Palestine.* There they formed the Polish Second Corps in the British Eighth Army and fought valiantly in the North African and Italian campaigns.

The British assumed that Polish servicemen would return home after the cessation of hostilities. Some did, and additional small numbers were repatriated to other countries, but more than half refused to leave. Many were afraid of reprisals if they returned; others simply had nowhere to return to, since most of eastern Poland was now part of the Soviet Union. Although the Polish government in exile had been "de-recognized" by the British government in July 1945, it stubbornly remained in place and continued

*One of the Polish soldiers was Menachem Begin. Like a number of Polish Jews, he deserted in Palestine and joined the Zionist resistance against the British.

to issue pronouncements. Polish commanders, particularly General Anders, were outspoken in their criticism of what they considered an illegitimate regime in Poland. While there was a lot of sympathy for the Soviet Union in Britain, the Poles were once more cast in the role of spoilers; according to a 1946 Gallup poll, less than a third of Britons agreed that the Poles should be allowed to remain. The Polish servicemen remembered Churchill telling the House of Commons: "His Majesty's Government will never forget the debt they owe to all the Polish troops who have served under our command, I earnestly hope that it may be possible to offer citizenship and freedom of the British Empire, if they so desire." Now they felt betrayed.*

Finally, after all attempts to encourage the Poles to leave failed, and as the harsh political reality in Poland became clearer, the British government relented. The Polish Resettlement Act of 1947 provided for payments to veterans who were disabled and to dependents of the deceased. Funds were allocated for temporary camps, and for health care and education. Polish doctors and pharmacists were given temporary licenses. Polish veterans were not granted citizenship, but they could apply for naturalization after five years. The most visible part of the pro-

*When the Russians insisted that Polish servicemen not be allowed to march in the victory parade held in London in 1946, the British agreed.

gram was the so-called Polish Resettlement Corps, a quasi-military organization in which the veterans, retaining their military rank and pay, were given language courses, vocational training, and time to look for work. After two years, they would be on their own. Given the impoverished state of the British postwar economy, this was generous.

My father was one of those who stayed. Unlike many, who were separated from their loved ones, he had his immediate family in England. Moreover, having served in the SOE, he had technically been a member of the Home Army, and he felt at particular risk if he returned to Poland. He joined the Resettlement Corps and was attached to an English manufacturer of electric railways. His work included planning rail lines in Brazil and India, and translating a German pamphlet on motor insulators.

After a year, still not demobilized, he was posted back to Scotland, to a Polish signals unit. This was discouraging, yet my father was luckier than most. He had been some time in England, spoke the language, and knew his way around; he had a family (three-quarters of the stranded Poles were men, most of them single); and he was able to continue in his prewar vocation and did not have to undergo retraining as a farm hand, factory worker, or coal miner, which were the British employment priorities. In addition, he had the funds to find private accommodations and did not have to live in a temporary camp. Yet his future was far from settled. He was thirty-eight. The Polish life that the war had taken away from him was in all ways much easier—a good job, assured social position, a wealthy father-in-law, a comfortable allowance, a settled future. At an age when most men are in mid-career, he was starting over—and in a foreign country. It was at that time that he developed what was diagnosed as a nervous stomach, probably an ulcer.

My father finally got his military discharge and was offered a teaching job. During the war, the Germans had closed all the universities in occupied Poland. To ensure some sort of continuity in intellectual life, the Polish government in London had established five teaching faculties, attached to various British universities. The plan was to transfer the personnel and students to Poland at the end of the war. When it became clear that this was not going to happen, the British government took over the program and closed all but the technical faculty, which was in London. Polish University College, or PUC (pronounced "poots" in Polish), had a thousand students enrolled in economics, architecture, and different branches of engineering, including electrical engineering, which my father taught.

Polish University College was part of the Polish émigré community in London. According to the 1951 Census, more than a third of the 140,000 Poles in Britain lived in London. Many refused to accept defeat. The remnant of the Polish general staff held itself in readiness, anticipating a war between the West and the Soviet Union. The Polish government in exile continued to issue communiqués criticizing the Soviet Union. Most Poles did what urban émigrés have always done—established a parallel homeland. They published newspapers and literary journals, ran bookstores and restaurants, and founded parishes, social clubs, and professional societies.

Life settled down for my parents. With four other Polish families, they bought a damaged house in Kensington, which they renovated. My father put his name down on a waiting list for a car—it took years for British postwar automobile production to catch up with demand. Meanwhile, like most people, we bicycled. We went on summer holidays to the seashore, Cornwall and Devon, camping or caravaning. After my brother was born, my parents sold their share of the Kensington house and, together with my father's mother, bought a small terrace house in the London suburb of New Malden, near Wimbledon, where eventually I went to school. I attended Donhead, a Jesuit preparatory school, wore a bright blue blazer and a blue schoolboy's cap. There was the occasional awkwardness of my unpronounceable name—or rather, my two unpronounceable names—but on the whole I fitted in.

I have a memory of that period. I am eight or nine, standing with other schoolboys on a green lawn, forming a large circle, maybe fifty feet across. In the center of the circle is a large cast-iron lawn roller. Somebody—our teacher?—throws a cricket ball at the roller, which causes it to bounce in unexpected directions. We have to catch the ball. I distinctly recall the metallic clunk of the hard leather striking the drum of the roller. I don't know why this moment made an impression on me—I don't have memories of being in the classroom, or of actually playing cricket. Perhaps it was taking part in a (slightly mysterious, to me) ritual, or the feeling of being accepted as one of the crowd, that impressed me.

Although my parents remained rooted in the Polish émigré community—my father was elected treasurer of the society of Polish electrical engineers, and my mother worked for a Polish medical association—they did not impose their Polishness on my brother and me. My father later told me that this was a conscious decision on their part. When the yoke of Stalinism descended on Poland in 1948, he took it for granted that we would never return, and he and my mother decided that my brother and I would be better off if we were not burdened with two cultures. I was not sent to Polish classes, or Polish Sunday school. I remember once being taken to the circus, but I don't recall any Polish events. I had no Polish friends. Nor was I taught to read and write in Polish. My favorite book was an illustrated annual of western movies—Lash La Rue and Tim Holt.

But although I wore a blazer and a schoolboy's cap, I wasn't really English. For one thing, I always spoke Polish with my parents, although I can't recall if I learned it first, or together with English. We also ate different foods, *barszcz* (beet soup) and *gołąbki* (stuffed cabbage rolls). At Christmastime we had *babka* instead of plum pudding, and jellied carp instead of roast beef. I got my presents on Christmas Eve instead of Christmas Day, and there was always something under my pillow on St. Nicholas Day. My parents continued the Polish custom of celebrating name days instead of birthdays. I always kissed my father on the cheek, not twice, as the French do, but three times, according to the Polish manner. Home is always a refuge from the outside world, but never more so than for the child of foreigners.

There was a catch to my father's job: PUC was temporary—the only students were Polish servicemen, and once they had completed their degrees, the university would close. In 1951, his final year of teaching, my father began to look for other work. He liked teaching and applied to universities in London, Manchester, and Newcastle, but without success. Like many of his friends—and many Englishmen—he began to think of emigrating. By this time he and my mother had applied for and been granted British citizenship, which gave them easy access to the countries of the British Commonwealth. My father wrote to universities in Australia, Canada, and Southern

Rhodesia, but without success. That year we spent the summer holidays camping in the French Alps with my uncle Marian and his wife, Ella. Somehow we all fitted into their small Opel. During the trip the two families decided that they would emigrate together. But where? Australia seemed too far, Africa was too unknown. They settled on Canada, specifically Quebec, since it was part French, and my uncle spoke French but not English.

At the last minute, my uncle and aunt changed their minds and decided to stay in Paris. In November 1952, my father sailed to Canada. The rest of the family would join him the following spring (my grandmother chose to stay in London). Arriving in Montreal, my father soon discovered that finding a university job was difficult, his limited teaching record in an unconventional institution not counting for much. His industrial experience in Poland and England proved useful, however, and after a few months of searching, he was hired by an electric cable manufacturing company located in St. Johns, a small town south of Montreal. The following April, my mother, my brother, and I sailed to Halifax on a venerable Cunard steamship, the *Franconia*.*

I don't remember much about the sea voyage. I

*The *Franconia* had a connection to Polish history. In 1945, she provided floating accommodations for Winston Churchill and the British delegation at Yalta, where the fate of central Europe—including Poland—was sealed.

generally suffer from seasickness, but I don't even recall that. I do remember an interminable train ride from Halifax to Montreal, through a forested landscape. Indeed, my distinct memories of childhood date mostly from after this time. It is as if England and Scotland had ceased to exist. I arrived in Canada speaking with an English accent, knowing the arcane rules of cricket, and wearing short pants (as all English schoolboys did). My first day of school, a fifth-grade classmate pointed at my shorts and said, "Do you ever look stupid." I put away my shorts and cricket skills, and learned to wear blue jeans and play hockey. It took a little longer to lose my English accent, but eventually that, too, disappeared.

Thus I became a Canadian or, rather, an English-speaking Quebecer. Although the province of Quebec was colonized by the French, hundreds of years ago, there were pockets of English-speaking population, dating back to the American War of Independence, when British loyalists fled north to safety. St. Johns was one of these settlements. The town had once been largely English, although it was now majority French.* There were no ethnic neighborhoods, but in most ways that mattered, French and English lived apart. Difference in language can be a

*In 1962, St. Johns was officially renamed Saint-Jean-sur-Richelieu.

formidable barrier, especially when that difference is institutionalized, as it was in Quebec. In St. Johns, children went to separate schools, families worshiped at separate churches, and people read different local newspapers, *Le Canada français* or *The News*. My father belonged to the Lions Club; if he had been French-speaking he might have joined the Société Saint-Jean-Baptiste. We all rooted for the Montreal Canadiens, though, who were also called *les habitants* (the original settlers of the province), or the Habs. This schizophrenic community was, altogether, an odd place.

I adapted easily to bifurcated St. Johns. I had grown up in two languages—Polish at home, English everywhere else—so having a third language on the periphery did not seem unusual. When my friends and I went to a double feature, it was to the "English" movie house, not to its "French" counterpart across the street. One of my favorite hangouts was a tobacconist shop on St. Jacques Street, whose interior smelled of cigarettes and newsprint. There were racks of newspapers and magazines brought—as I imagined it—from the four corners of the world. That was where I bought my copies of *MAD* and *Railroad Model Craftsman*. There must have been French-Canadian magazines and newspapers in the racks as well, but I never noticed them. That was not my world. Similarly, I skipped over the French channels on our new television set and watched *Have*

Gun—Will Travel and *The Ed Sullivan Show* on the American stations (we were only twenty miles from the border).

There was a pool hall and bowling alley on St. Johns's main street that catered to everyone, but we did not mingle. I didn't know any French-Canadians in the town; all my friends were English-speaking. In the summer, we would go to the grandly named St. Johns Yacht Club (there were no boats, let alone yachts, it was a swimming pier jutting into the Richelieu River); young French Canadians would go upstream to the OTJ. L'Oeuvre des Terrains de Jeux (or the Playground Society) had been founded by lay clergy and was operated under the auspices of the Roman Catholic Church. The Church was a social, political, and economic power in the province. Religious orders ran most of the French-speaking schools, colleges, universities, and hospitals, and Roman Catholicism was, for all practical purposes, the state religion. The most prominent civic buildings in St. Johns were large stone parish churches, and the largest complex in town, second in size only to the Singer sewing machine factory, was a seminary.

We lived near the seminary, on the edge of town and next to open countryside. My best friend was Gareth Harding, whose home was nearby, and whose father taught English literature at the Royal Military College. Gareth introduced me to bird watching. Together, we roamed the nearby fields and woods, building forts and treetop lookouts. Some children played cowboys and Indians; we played war. I had a toy six-shooter that could be loaded with a paper roll of gunpowder caps, and when it worked, which was irregularly, made a sharp crack and produced a wonderful acrid smell of burning black powder. I carried it in my father's old leather army holster. My favorite weapon was a Sten gun that I made myself out of a piece of steel pipe taped to a wooden stock. It didn't look very real, but it was realistically heavy. Of course, I had to supply the ack-ack sound of a machine pistol myself, but that was a satisfying part of the game. That and falling dramatically to the ground when you were hit.

I didn't associate war with death. My uncle Marian survived his time as a German prisoner of war, and he joked about the experience. A friend of my parents had a concentration camp number tattooed on her arm, and I knew that something horrible had happened to her, although I never heard her speak of it. But none of our immediate family had died in the war. I suppose I'm excusing my fascination with things military, but in an odd way, while I knew that war was destructive, it didn't seem deadly.

The first book I remember that gave me a taste for literature was *The Last of the Mohicans,* a war story if ever there was one. Before Fenimore Cooper I read many of G. A. Henty's boys' books—he wrote about eighty of them, mostly in the early 1900s. The English writer's novels were not assigned reading, but I came across a whole shelf of them in my school library and enthusiastically worked my way down the row.* George Alfred Henty had served in the Crimean War and later been a war correspondent, and the youthful protagonists of his stories were invariably caught up in armed conflicts, usually in the far reaches of the British Empire. Henty, an imperialist, was catholic in his choice of subjects, and in addition to *With Wolfe in Canada,* and *With Clive in India,* he wrote *With Lee in Virginia,* and *Out with Garibaldi.* I liked the stories, and also the books themselves, sturdy Edwardian products with richly embossed leather covers instead of flimsy dust jackets.

In adolescence I gobbled up C. S. Forester's Horatio Hornblower series, which was set against the background of the Napoleonic wars. I haven't reread Forester's books since, so I don't know how he stacks up against Patrick O'Brian's masterful maritime novels, but Hornblower occupies a special place in my imagination. Not only because he got there first but also because his books are jumbled together with memories of a 1950s movie (starring Gregory Peck) and a long-running radio program.

*Had I been forced to read Henty, would I have discovered Dickens?

"Set top gallants, if you please, Mr. Bush!" I listened late at night, lying in bed in the dark, the ideal setting for storytelling.

When I was fourteen, for the first and only time, I was sent to summer camp. It was a Polish boys' camp—my parents must have decided that I needed some formal exposure to my heritage after all. Located in the Laurentian Mountains north of Montreal, it was called a scout camp, but the councilors were all Polish ex-army men who ran it like basic training. We were issued khaki uniforms and slept on canvas cots in army-surplus tents. I was in the Boy Scouts and had been on overnight outings, but this was different. Instead of camp projects we built log bridges, instead of games there were obstacle courses and maneuvers in the surrounding woods. It was my last brush with the martial arts.

My Two Polish Grandfathers

My parents' lives in a faraway country were the subjects of family stories, which were told and retold like fairy tales. The leading characters were my banker grandfather, Mieczysław Jan Hofman (left), and my scientist grandfather, Witold Erasmus Rybczyński.

When I was a boy, conversations around the kitchen table were regularly punctuated by the phrase *przed wojną*—before the war. My parents' lives in a faraway country were the subjects of family stories, which were told and retold like fairy tales. Once upon a time there was a place where everyone was happy all the time, living in splendid houses, going to balls, finding glass slippers. In the fairy tales, the war was like the evil witch: malevolent, destructive, ruinous. The stories had different purposes. For my parents, they kept alive the memory of who they were—or had been. But the tales were also for the benefit of my brother and me. Of course, the subjects of my parents' stories were people who, in most cases, were still alive, but to me they seemed as distant as ancient ancestors. And just as potent.

My mother's fairy tale involved growing up in an enchanted castle. The family house was on Mokotowska Street, near the city's principal park, Łazienki Gardens, and behind Aleje Ujazdowskie, a broad avenue with parallel rows of lime trees—Warsaw's Champs-Elysées. The neoclassic house was designed by Francesco Maria Lanci, one of those itinerant Italian architects common in nineteenth-century central Europe.* Lanci had built the house in 1860 for Józef Ignacy Kraszewski, the foremost Polish man of letters of his time. My grandfather bought it in 1928 and spent two years renovating and enlarging; with three daughters, he needed more space. The building was laid out like a Renaissance villa,

*Lanci spent his whole professional life in Poland. The house on Mokotowska Street was one of his last projects, and was finished by his architect-son, named Witold.

with high-ceilinged living quarters on the second floor and lower-ceilinged service rooms below. The family occupied only the upper floor, the lower level was rented for offices, and the cellar contained rooms for storing coal, potatoes, pickle barrels, and wine. The household staff included a nanny, two maids, a cook, and a watchman who tended the furnace. My mother, her older sister, Wisia, and their little brother, Michał, who was born the year they moved in, all had their own bedrooms, which seemed luxurious to me since my brother and I shared a room. Krysia, the youngest sister, slept in her mother's room; my grandfather had his own room as well as a library—he was an avid reader. There was a small salon and a large drawing room for entertaining, as well as a long dining room with heavy oak furniture. Outside the dining room was a terrace with an ivy-covered stair leading to the garden. The garden, which was overlooked by four-story apartment blocks, was not large, and on hot summer days the family decamped to a country house in Piaseczno, a small town in the Warsaw suburbs. There, while the accommodations were rude, without indoor plumbing or running water, the girls and their friends could enjoy a modern amenity: a tennis court. Lazy summers in the country, a bustling household in town—it all sounds wonderfully civilized.

The walls of the entrance hall at Mokotowska Street were hung with animal trophies—stags' antlers and boars' tusks—for my grandfather's other passion was hunting. The extensive wilderness areas of rural Poland offered a wealth of opportunities. There were boar in the *puszcza*, or primeval forest, in national parks on the Lithuanian border, deer in the Carpathian Mountains, waterfowl in the Pripet Marshes, and hunting clubs stocked with partridge and wood grouse in the vicinity of Warsaw. These outings were generally social occasions, groups of men setting out in horse-drawn carriages—or a convoy of cars—carrying hampers of food and drink. Hunts on private estates were sometimes followed by house parties, to which nonhunters—and wives—were invited. One of the hunting trophies on the wall at Mokotowska Street included a gold medal from the 1937 International Hunting Exhibition in Berlin.* That event was presided over by another enthusiastic hunter, Hermann Göring.

My grandfather Mieczysław Jan Hofman was, in every sense, a self-made man. He was born in 1881 in Kalisz, a small city west of Warsaw on the Prosna River, which, until the end of the First World War, marked the boundary between the Russian and the Prussian parts of Poland, Kalisz being on the eastern (Russian) bank. He was the son of a customs official

*When the house was requisitioned by the occupying German army, the officer in charge, a hunter himself and impressed by the gold medal, provided the family alternative accommodations.

whose father had migrated from Bavaria to be manager of a local estate, and had set down roots and assimilated.* As a young man, my grandfather studied economics in St. Petersburg, the capital of the Russian Empire. The choice of the distant university was a measure of his ambition. Although he came from a solidly middle-class family—one brother became an engineer, another a pharmacist—he chose to make his own way, leaving home at an early age and supporting himself as a student by managing investments for wealthy clients. He clearly had a head for business, and on his return, he worked for—and ended up running—a cooperative savings bank based in Poznań. He then became president of Bank Handlowy (Commerce Bank), the largest privately-owned bank in the country, headquartered in Warsaw. My grandfather belonged to what Poles call the "generation of the twenties," that is, the generation responsible for building the modern Polish state after the rebirth of the republic in 1918 (Bank Handlowy, for example, financed the construction of Gdynia, Poland's only Baltic port). He married Jadwiga Głowacka, the daughter of a Lublin judge, and had a happy family life including—and how important this was at that time—a male heir. He

*Partitioned Poland was a mixture of many peoples. The spoken languages, in addition to Polish, Russian, and German, included Ukrainian, Lithuanian, Czech, Silesian, Belarusan, Kashubian, Slovak, Romany, and Yiddish.

was fifty when he moved into the house on Mokotowska Street. In other words, a classic success story.

My grandfather appears somewhat forbidding in photographs, with a notable exception. A snapshot shows him sitting on a garden bench with another man. Jerzy Komorowski was president of the largest steel works and machine factory in Poland, Lilpop, Rau & Loewenstein (for whom my father worked). The two men were best friends, had lunch once a week at a Warsaw businessmen's club, and went hunting together. The extensive garden in the photo is behind Komorowski's summer house; the time is late spring of that fateful Polish year, 1939. The two friends are smoking—an ashtray between them—relaxed and smiling; perhaps the photographer has just said something funny. Or maybe they are amused at the odd spectacle they make. My grandfather is wearing a tweed suit, white shirt, and natty bow tie. He seems to have dropped in unannounced, for Komorowski is casually dressed, in a sort of T-shirt, white shorts, socks rolled down to his ankles, and—a jarring note—beat-up leather brogues. It's what one might wear on a Saturday morning for a spot of gardening. Yet despite, or perhaps because of, their contrasting dress, the two figures make a definite pair. An odd couple, one might say: the industrialist, relaxed, expansive, apparently uninhibited; the banker, more compact and controlled, not aloof, exactly, but with something held in reserve.

I never knew my grandfather, who died when I was a year old. He knew of me, however. In his will he left me, his only grandson, a share in one of his apartment buildings, the equivalent of the not inconsiderable sum of twenty-five thousand zlotys. He wrote the will in December 1943. By then, his stocks and bonds—he patriotically invested only in Polish companies—had been rendered worthless by the war. In addition to making various provisions for his family, the will also specified two scholarships at Warsaw's business school for the children of bank employees. "I acquired my estate by the work and savings of my entire life," my grandfather wrote, "for I inherited nothing from my parents and did not accept a dowry when I married." But the three-page handwritten document offers a glimpse of something else beneath the severity. After precisely spelling out the legal details of his bequests, he added a touching message to his family, written in a formal, old-fashioned Polish that doesn't quite translate into English.

I strongly ask my wife to continue to safeguard the children's welfare, to assist them morally as well as materially, and to bring up Michał as a brave and patriotic citizen. As for the children, they should try, during all their lives, to be modest and true in order to stay cheerful in heart and mind, to work and save, not only for themselves but, as far as pos-

sible, for the entire community, and to love and help one another. Be happy, my dear ones, and may God bless you.

He scrawled a terse postscript untidily at the bottom of the page: "Due to completely altered circumstances I hereby annul this will." He added that on October 24, 1944, on his deathbed. The altered circumstances to which he alluded were the result of the Warsaw uprising. When the city fell, and the Germans ordered an evacuation, half a million Varsovians were interned in Durchgangslager 121, a transit camp at Pruszków, a Warsaw suburb. From there, they were sent either to work on fortifications outside the city, to Germany as forced labor, or to concentration camps. My grandfather bribed a guard to let his family out of the camp and, hidden in hay wagons, they made their way to a friend's country estate. From there they could hear the boom of detonations as the Germans blew up the city, block after block, building after building.

Before leaving his house on Mokotowska Street, my grandfather had concealed two suitcases containing gold coins, the family silver, a collection of pocket watches, and the deeds to his properties—all that was left of his fortune—in a bricked-up room in the cellar. Since access to the city was forbidden, he hired two men to retrieve the valuables. They did so, but when he opened the suitcases, they contained only bundles of old newspapers; someone—most likely the hired men—had removed the contents. Faced with this ultimate indignity, my grandfather collapsed with a stroke, and died a day later.

I never warmed to my mother's tale. It seemed to me sad—a tale of loss rather than accomplishment. Moreover, the grand house on Mokotowska Street served only to underline the modesty of our own suburban lives: our small home, our unexceptional recreations, our holidays spent in rented caravans or in crowded campgrounds. No hunting parties or balls, or private tennis courts. It made my grandfather's achievement sound even more distant, and more unreal.

My father's fairy tale was about his father the schoolteacher—except he wasn't, exactly. Witold Erasmus Rybczyński was also born in 1881, but at the other end of the country, in Stanisławów, a small town in the Austrian province of Galicia. Despite the exotic name, Galicia was a backwater of the Habsburg Empire, and, like much of central Europe, it was a cultural stew. The two largest groups, separated by language, religion, and culture, were the Polish landowners and city dwellers, and the Ruthenian peasantry, who were known as Little Russians and were descendants of the ancient Kievan Ruś. The cities contained sizable Jewish communities as well as a small number of German and Austrian civil servants. With the exception of the townspeople, and a handful of Polish aristocrats, the inhabitants of this largely agricultural area were poor, so poor indeed that, according to the historian Norman Davies, "Galicia was in a worse predicament than Ireland at the start of the potato famine."

The two main cities of Galicia were Krakau and Lemberg—Kraków and Lwów to the Poles—which were the capitals of the western and eastern parts of the province. Despite the rural poverty around them, the cities were prosperous. Lemberg was a charming place, with a cobblestone market square, beautiful Baroque churches, and a Viennese-style opera house. The Habsburgs' policy of benevolent neglect allowed Polish institutions to thrive (German and Polish were the official languages), and among Lemberg's cultural institutions was the venerable university where my grandfather studied philosophy. His doctoral diploma, in physics and mathematics, was awarded by Emperor Franz Joseph I and includes the title of the dissertation: "The Movement of a Fluid Sphere in a Viscous Liquid Under the Influence of Gravity."

I have his photograph, a studio portrait, probably taken when he was in his twenties. He is a handsome man, with a mustache and long sideburns, dressed for the occasion in a dark vested suit. He is wearing a high starched collar with a diamond stickpin through the knot of his silk tie, which is fashionably loose. He looks ambitious, studious, and quietly self-confident. His father was a district court judge and a leading citizen in the small country town of Kolomya. He must have been prosperous, for he sent both his sons to university. After my grandfather graduated, he married Kazimiera Łaska, a young woman from an established Lemberg family, and the following year they had a son. Their apartment, on Castle Hill, overlooked the city. For the next five years my grandfather taught in a *gimnazium,* or high school, and continued his research in theoretical physics. Secondary education was a serious business in the Austrian Empire, with teaching ranks as in a university, and in due course he was promoted to professor. His doctoral thesis was translated into several languages. Like most Galician intellectuals, he looked beyond his homeland. The University of Lemberg was well regarded abroad, and he received a scholarship to work under the great theoretical physicist Arnold Sommerfeld at the University of Munich, and for several years lived with his wife and young son in Germany, where he also met Max Planck and Albert Einstein.

The family summered in Jaremcze, a village in the Carpathian Mountains, south of Lemberg. They were there in August 1914, when the First World War broke out. Barely escaping the Russian invasion, they fled west through Hungary to Vienna, where they spent most of the war. Although my grandfather had done his compulsory military service, a weak heart prevented him from being conscripted. Instead, he worked for an organization that helped refugees, of whom there were many, for Galicia was a chief theater of the Eastern Front and the fighting was fierce, especially around the fortress town of Lemberg. At first the Russians were successful and overran the city, but following the abdication of the czar and the Bolshevik coup, their army crumbled and Austro-German troops advanced deep into Ukraine. In 1917, after the Russian rout, my grandparents were able to move back to Galicia, though not to Lemberg but to Tarnów, a small country town in the western part of the province, where my grandfather had relatives.

At the end of the war, the situation in Lemberg remained tense. The defeat of the Germans and the collapse of the Habsburg Empire produced chaos in Galicia, as it did throughout central Europe. Polish and Ruthenian nationalists both occupied parts of the city, and the Ruthenians proclaimed a republic allied with the neighboring short-lived Ukrainian People's Republic. Meanwhile the newly formed Polish state claimed Galicia as its own. The Polish army occupied Lemberg in short order, and after eight months of fighting established control over the entire province. By then my grandmother and her son were back in Lwów, as it was now called. They lived with her parents, but without my grandfather, who had stayed in Tarnów. Their marriage was over.

My grandfather spent the rest of his life in Tarnów. He got a job in the local *gimnazium* and never returned to Lwów, or to the cosmopolitan world of theoretical physics. One day he was a budding young physicist (just before the war he had been offered a teaching chair at the university), the next he was teaching the second law of thermodynamics to country lads. Fairy tales do not have to explain events; things just happen—the bean is planted and the stalk grows—so my grandfather's odd decision was never clearly explained. It was only much later that I pieced together what may have happened. My grandfather—he was thirty-seven—had fallen in love. Marja Vayhinger was the lonely and unhappy wife of a local government official who traveled a lot (he was in charge of locks and waterways in the district). He must have been a tolerant sort, for my grandfather became a frequent houseguest, although the precise nature of Marja and his relationship remains unclear. They lived together for more than thirty years, but as lovers or platonic friends? They never married. Yet the fact remains that he gave up everything for her: wife, family, career.

Marja must have felt guilty about breaking up the marriage, for she introduced my now-divorced grandmother to her brother, Adam Korytowski, a former captain in the Austrian cavalry, now a major in the new Polish army. The major proposed, and Kazimiera accepted. My father never talked about why his parents divorced, and Marja was never mentioned, except in passing, and then only as the sister of his stepfather. As a boy, I was given to understand, in some vague way, that it was my grandmother who was to blame for the breakup. From the time she lived with us in England, I have vague memories of *babcia's* bedroom, which I was sometimes allowed to visit. The darkened room had for me a dissolute air, not only because she had divorced—which I knew was forbidden by the Church—but also because she was the only one in the house who smoked. She used a holder and had a snuffer shaped like the famous statue of the Belgian Boy. I think it was this—the smoking and the little peeing boy—that made her supposed culpability easy for me to accept.

What my father did recount, with obvious affection, were his boyhood summer holidays with his father, whom he revered. These periods were spent not in Tarnów but in Lusławice, a nearby village in the Carpathian foothills. Here the Vayhingers owned a summer residence, an early-nineteenth-century manor house on the Dunajec River. A prominent figure in the Lusławice fairy tale was Jacek Malczewski, a painter. In 1921, at the age of sixty-seven, Malczewski moved his family from

Kraków to Lusławice, where his two sisters lived. By then he was Poland's most renowned painter and Marja Vayhinger, in the guise of patroness, built him a studio on her estate. He painted there for the next five years and was a regular visitor at the manor house. An ascetic-looking man with gaunt features and a beard (there are many self-portraits, one in a suit of armor that makes him look like Don Quixote), he painted allegorical scenes in a realistic style, peopling the Polish countryside with biblical and mystical figures. He made a small painting of my grandfather. It is a simple scene: my grandfather and Marja's son, Adzio, on a tennis court, the two standing figures in crisp white shirts with rolled sleeves, my grandfather holding a racket. Although Malczewski's work tends to be melancholy, the atmosphere here is cheerfully summery, the afternoon sun low, the chirping of the crickets almost audible.

I was much taken with my grandfather's story—the romantic liaison, the mysterious retreat from a scientific career, life in a secluded country manor, rubbing shoulders with a famous painter. The fact that I was his namesake made this particular fairy tale even more appealing.

My grandfather retired from teaching in 1933, at the age of only fifty-two, supposedly the result of his weak heart. Or maybe he just wanted to stop. A former student remembered him as his best teacher, and an outstanding public lecturer, but not someone who seemed to be absorbed by teaching. His students liked him, but he kept his distance—both from them and from other teachers. A colleague described him as spending his free time at home, surrounded by books and paintings. After retirement he devoted himself to reading and writing—his eclectic works included many poems, a physics textbook, numerous magazine articles, a translation of Maeterlinck's *Death*, and a popular scientific book titled *What Is Radar?* He and Marja now lived at Lusławice together year-round—she had separated from her husband. My mother remembers visiting them on the occasion of her marriage. She recalls that they addressed each other formally, *pan* and *pani*—sir and madam. My mother did not know her father-in-law well, but he struck her as a gentle, retiring, and content person; she remembers Marja, who was known as Nunia, as a commanding presence who looked like George Sand.

My father's last summer in Lusławice was in 1939, just before the outbreak of the Second World War. The Germans occupied Galicia, but fighting generally bypassed the isolated village. Marja and my grandfather stayed in the house, taking in a score of displaced relatives and friends. He went back to teaching—clandestinely, for schools were outlawed. After the end of the war, eastern Galicia became part of the Union of Soviet Socialist Republics, with

Galician Poles forcibly resettled and Lwów renamed L'viv. Western Galicia—and Lusławice—remained in what was now the People's Republic of Poland. Marja and my grandfather continued to live in the old manor house, where he died in 1949. While playing bridge, he bent down to retrieve a dropped card, and his heart just stopped. He was buried in the village cemetery, less than two hundred miles from where he was born, yet, in its own way, the trajectory of his life was as roiled by external events as that of his son. He sampled all the forms of government that the turbulent twentieth century had to offer: imperial rule under the Habsburgs; democracy and then authoritarianism during the twenty-year Polish Republic; fascism under the Third Reich's General Gouvernement; and—briefly—Communism. In spite—or, perhaps, because—of the unsettled times in which he lived, he created for himself a remarkably settled existence. His was a happy unhappy life, which, as John Lukacs has pointed out, is preferable to an "unhappy happy one."

I once visited Lusławice. Tarnów, where my grandfather had taught school, was a sleepy country town, just as I had imagined. A local bus dropped me at the hamlet of Lusławice, and I easily found the manor house, a rustic Palladian villa with an elegant central portico supported by Doric columns. The large grounds were overgrown, and the building was boarded up. I walked up the road and, after asking directions, located the local cemetery. The graves were scattered beneath a grove of trees. I found my grandfather's tombstone; it gave me a frisson to read his/my name. It was a hot summer's day, but cool in the dark shade. All around was a rolling landscape of open fields and meadows, bright in the glaring sun.

Part II

July 1964. Architectural travel is a long-standing tradition that derives from the so-called Grand Tour of the eighteenth and nineteenth centuries, when young British gentlemen traveled Europe in a sort of educational rite of passage. My tour took me to the ancient city of Pompeii; Michael Rain (left) was an English actor whom I met on the boat from Patras.

Music

August 1913. My father, who began studying music at the age of five, playing four-handed piano with his father in their summer house at Jaremcze in the Carpathian Mountains.

My childhood contained many traces of Poland—language, cuisine, family stories—and my father's piano playing. He had grown up in a musical household. His father was a self-taught pianist, and his mother a trained musician who studied at the Lemberg Conservatory and was an accompanist as well as a piano teacher. My father began playing at five, and at eight, while the family was living in Vienna, he was sent to the conservatory. He continued formal studies throughout his high school years and was enrolled at the Warsaw Conservatory when he began classes in engineering at the Technical University. Then, abruptly, he dropped out of the music program.

He never explained his decision not to pursue a musical career—surely his mother's hope—except to say that he found it impossible to study simultaneously music and engineering. Perhaps he was rebelling. Music may have been a sore point between mother and son, for during all the time my grandmother lived with us in England, I never once heard her play the piano, nor did she undertake to give me piano lessons, despite that having been her métier. But I may be reading too much into all this. After an unsettled childhood, perhaps my father simply preferred a more stable profession to the vagaries and uncertainties of a musical life. He may have felt himself temperamentally ill-suited to the pressures of the concert stage, or believed that he lacked sufficient talent. The latter reason would not have occurred to me; I was proud of his playing. I remember an absurd but intense argument with a schoolmate on the subject of who was a better pianist, my father or Liberace.

Whatever the reason for my father's choice, he did not give up playing the piano—far from it. He continued taking private lessons. After graduating, he performed publicly as part of a duo, had a monthly hour-long program of light music on the radio, and wrote and arranged songs for a female vocal trio with whom he performed in local cabarets. The demands of married life cramped his performing career, but wartime, if anything, revived it. The young Polish lieutenant who could play Gershwin's "Rhapsody in Blue" as well as Chopin mazurkas was greatly in demand. While training with the parachute battalion in Scotland, he performed in local town halls and movie theaters, in Christmas shows for servicemen, at dancing parties for the Polish-Scottish Society, and formed a duo with Flick McIntyre, a soprano Wren. His solo repertoire included not only classical composers but also the tearful "Warsaw Concerto," which had recently appeared as a film score in the immensely popular *Dangerous Moonlight*. Nor did the playing stop when he was stationed in Italy. He performed for the FANY girls during musical evenings at the Bazall base in Latiano. While he was in the Polish Resettlement Corps, he teamed up again with McIntyre, entering a talent competition and placing second. Wherever he was, he had his music, which was both a social passport and a touchstone in an upside-down life.

What did you do in the war, Daddy? I played. There are worse answers. In old World War II movies, there is sometimes a musical interlude between action scenes, when a group of tough, weary soldiers gathers around a piano. One of them plays, the rest sing along, their faces reflecting thoughts of loved ones and home far away. The piano player is never the star of the movie, but in that scene, at least, he is the center of attention.

When my father returned to England from his SOE posting in Italy, one of the first things he did was to buy a secondhand piano. It must have been a poor instrument, for only two years later he replaced it with an old Schubach, purchased with his demobilization pay—one hundred pounds. He tuned it himself, using a wrench made out of a Sten gun barrel. He occasionally performed in public, sometimes played when we had company, and every year played Polish carols after *wigilia,* the ceremonial Christmas Eve meal. But mostly—daily—he played for himself. This was usually in the evenings, after the dinner things had been put away. Warming up with scales, he would go on for an hour or so, Beethoven, Schumann, Debussy, but mostly—although I did not know this at the time—Chopin. I would regularly fall asleep to the sound of his playing.

I never learned to play the piano. My father gave me lessons when I was twelve, but they did not take. Musical notation eluded me, and I got bored playing scales—who doesn't? Perhaps I didn't have any talent, or perhaps I was simply too old—at twelve, my father had already composed his first mazurka. "My mother pushed me into it," he used to say wryly. Evidently, the memory was not an entirely happy one and he didn't want me to relive it, for my lessons were soon discontinued.

It was not until high school that I was drawn to music. I attended Loyola College High School, a Jesuit boys' school in Montreal, to which I commuted daily by train from St. Johns. The school had been founded by four Irish priests, and the majority of the students—and many of the teachers—were of Irish descent; the rest of us were of Italian and central European stock, with a sprinkling of Latin Americans. There were also French Canadians—Dick Seguin, Mike Gendron, John Bourque—although we always addressed one another in English and I did not think of them as French, any more than I thought of Pat Kenniff as Irish, or Vic Pappalardo as Italian.

The curriculum was firmly grounded in the three Rs—actually the four Rs, since we also had a course in religion. We studied mathematics intensively, Latin for four years, and knew all the world capitals. Of the physical sciences we had only a smattering—I never mixed chemicals or dissected frogs. Learning was by rote (I can still recite a good part of Longfellow's "The Wreck of the Hesperus"), classes were large (between thirty and forty) and discipline strict. Inattention in class could get you a chalk projectile between the ears; sloppy homework was punished by a session of "jug," or study hall; more serious infractions, such as running in the hall, could get you paddled—on the open palm. In other words, it was the opposite of modern pedagogical theory, and on the whole it worked admirably.

The Jesuits' idea of a well-rounded education extended beyond schoolwork. Each of the four years had several classes, which competed in a variety of mostly team sports. Over the years, I played football, basketball, volleyball, softball, hockey, and tennis, as well as swimming and track and field, which meant that I missed only skiing (I lived too far away to go on day trips to the Laurentian Mountains) and golf. My favorite sport was floor hockey, a lethal indoor Canadian version played on a basketball court with a puck that resembled a felt doughnut and a short piece of broom handle that served alternately as hockey stick and cudgel. The aim of all this athleticism was to burn off youthful energy, of course, but also to build character and self-discipline. Or, as an epigram in one of the annual yearbooks baldly put it: "Teach children that their primary difficulty will be, not with use of intelligence, but with control of the inherited brute in their natures."

Civilizing us little brutes took different forms. In between locker-room showers, I attended meetings of the math club, built sets for a theater production of *Billy Budd*, and was assistant editor of *The*

Inkwell, a class paper. I wrote quite a lot in high school—for the yearbook and for a literary magazine—although I never joined the brainier boys on the staff of the school newspaper or in the debating society. The only thing missing from this rich extracurricular mix was music; there was no marching band, no school orchestra, not even a choir. As far as music was concerned, the "Jebbies" were stone-deaf.

I have often met people whose education by priests or nuns has left them with a bitter taste. That was not my experience. Most of my teachers were Jesuits. I never found them forbidding, except perhaps Father Casey, our principal, a serious man who resembled T. E. Lawrence. I quickly learned that beneath their uniform black cassocks, my teachers were varied individuals—avuncular, witty, extroverted, caustic, severe, shy. What they all shared was a penetrating and challenging intelligence, and a lifelong dedication to teaching boys. The reputation of Roman Catholic priests with respect to boys lies in tatters today. All I can say is that in the 1950s, in my school, there was no hint of impropriety.

In addition to the permanent faculty of older priests, there was a rotating cadre of young men in their twenties who were scholastics, or priests-in-training. At that time, the Jesuit preparation for ordination lasted thirteen years and included, at midpoint, a three-year teaching stint in one of the fifty-odd Jesuit high schools in Canada and the United States. Scholastics wore cassocks and clerical collars but were addressed as "Mister" not "Father," and, being closer in age to ourselves, they were often our favorites. Garry Wills, who was a Jesuit novice in the 1950s, has observed about scholastics that these "young idealists still on their way to the priesthood offered stirring models for their students, who wanted to join them in their high calling." Stirring models, indeed. I recall a class outing to a rural area near a Mohawk reservation. We rowed leaky boats along the shore of the St. Lawrence River, water slopping over the gunwales. At one point a group of native boys started pelting us with stones. Mr. M., the scholastic overseeing our trip, rallied our forces and instigated a counterattack. He might have reminded us—though he didn't—that the Iroquois and the Black Robes had a long and bitter history of feuding.

Four figures personified the school's teaching philosophy: Father Casey, the principal, oversaw matters of the intellect; Father McGinnis, the prefect of discipline, kept order and administered the occasional paddling; Mr. Meagher, the athletic director—a lay teacher—saw to our bodies; and Father Devlin, the spiritual director, took care of our souls. Father Devlin's bailiwick included the Sodality of Our Lady, a Jesuit institution founded on religious exercises and private devotions. There were sixty or seventy so-called Sodalists in a school of five hundred, so we thought of ourselves as a spiritual elite—the Virgin Mary's Special Forces. Although I was devout, I never considered the priesthood for myself. It wasn't that I didn't respect my robed teachers, or their way of life, but I assumed a vocation would come in a flash of blinding light—and that never happened to me.

Spiritual development notwithstanding, there was one thing even more exclusive than being a Sodalist, and that was being a Loyola Warrior, a member of the school football team. My friend Frank Meagher was the star tackle. Despite my involvement in sports, I wasn't a natural athlete, so I was flattered by his friendship. Frank was older than I, having been kept back a year—the Jesuits didn't believe in social promotion, and boys regularly failed. As fifteen-year-olds sometimes do, I took my older friend as a model, copying his mannerisms, mimicking his jokes. I even went so far as to try out for the football team. I was tall for my age, but I had played only touch football, so I was unprepared for the rough-and-tumble of the game; moreover, having started out playing rugby, I had a poor grasp of the rules. I was eliminated on the first cut.

Frank was not an academic standout, but neither was he a typical jock, for he was an accomplished drummer. That was something I could do, I thought. He gave me a pair of old drumsticks and recommended a Gene Krupa exercise book. I started by playing paradiddles on a rubber pad and later bought a snare drum and a high hat from a pawnshop on Montreal's Craig Street. At about the same time—I'm not sure which came first—I became interested in jazz. This interest, which did not come from Frank, probably started as an act of adolescent rebellion, since my father played and listened only to classical music. I bought my first jazz record album, *Count 'Em 88,* on the strength of the odd title and the cover art—a photograph of a white grand piano. The trio was led by a twenty-six-year-old pianist, Ahmad Jamal. It was a lucky choice, for Jamal is an exceptional musician who plays a delicate and subtle form of jazz. I went on from there to the rhythmic intricacies of the Dave Brubeck Quartet, the jumpy bebop of Miles Davis, and the West Coast cool of Gerry Mulligan. I didn't just listen to the music. When there was no one at home, I would set up a record on my father's hi-fi and drum along, more or less imitating, as best I could, Philly Joe Jones or Shelly Manne.

Jazz was a private pastime, since none of my friends listened to the music. Making my own way was part of the pleasure. St. Johns did not have a jazz club, but the tobacconist's shop did carry *Down Beat.* The magazine was like a jazz correspondence course. It was also—and this was part of the attraction—an escape from a sometimes dreary and always provincial town.

Jazz was the music of big cities, especially one big city: New York. In *Down Beat* I read about a famed New York jazz club, Birdland—named after Charlie "Yardbird" Parker, the legendary alto saxophonist who had played at its opening a decade earlier. According to the magazine, Birdland had a special section reserved for underage patrons like me—I was sixteen. So, when my family went on a Christmas holiday to New York City, after we visited Radio City Music Hall, the Empire State Building, and a Horn & Hardart Automat, I knew exactly where I wanted to go. Actually, my first musical destination was a Harry Belafonte concert, hardly an original choice—his record had just become the world's first million-selling LP. Since my parents didn't share my interest in calypso, I went alone. All I remember today is that I sat in the back of the very large theater, and that Belafonte wore extremely brightly colored shirts. The following evening, having proved that I could be trusted, I was allowed to venture out again. We were staying at a seedy hotel near Times Square, and I set off up Broadway to Fifty-second Street. It was a day or two before New Year's Eve, and the city was in a festive mood. Many of the bars were open to the street, and people and music spilled out on the sidewalk. The noise, the neon lights, and the crowd were exhilarating and not the least threatening. It was December 1959.

When I reached Birdland, I felt slightly let down.

The basement club, with no marquee and no grand entrance, didn't look like a jazz Mecca. I tried to appear nonchalant as I went in. Just as *Down Beat* had described, I was shown to a raised section in the rear of the dark room and served a soft drink. It was early in the evening, and no one was playing. Eventually, musicians filed up onto the stage, spotlights were turned on, and with the arrival of the man himself—Count Basie—the sound of a big band at full tilt filled the room.

For once, the hackneyed phrase is apt: I was blown away. I had listened to records on my father's hi-fi, but the only live jazz I had ever heard was a performance by Benny Goodman in the Montreal Forum: swing music in a cavernous space. I was unprepared for the visceral impact of a hard-driving band in a small room. Nor had I ever heard anyone sing like Joe Williams—my parents' taste in popular crooners ran to Perry Como. I stayed for two sets. I don't recall the walk back to the hotel. After Basie, Broadway seemed pretty tame.

My father didn't accompany me to Birdland, but several times in Montreal we did go to jazz concerts together, not only Goodman but also the Modern Jazz Quartet and Duke Ellington. These occasions were memorable because it was rare that the two of us went out. It's not that we didn't spend time together, but it was usually with the rest of the family, on vacations, camping trips, outings. He was a private man and, with me at least, somewhat remote. This remoteness was probably unintentional—he suffered the disadvantage of many immigrant fathers: his boyhood had been so different from his son's. The things that he had done as an adolescent—kayaking, spending summers at country houses, going to formal social functions, giving piano recitals—were not things I did. The books he read as a boy were not my own (I could not read Polish). Playing the piano was his sole pastime, so he did not have any hobbies to share—he was not a fisherman, or a golfer, or a do-it-yourselfer—nor did we go to baseball or hockey games together. I don't mean to sound rueful. Despite my schoolboy athleticism, I was not attracted by the spectacle of sports, so I didn't feel I was missing anything.

My father and I did share something in addition to the occasional jazz concert. For some reason he did not introduce me to classical music—except indirectly through his evening playing—but we did sometimes play at home together. Like many classically trained musicians, he was somewhat baffled by the improvisational nature of jazz, but he did know how to improvise fugues. I enjoyed accompanying him, although I'm not sure if he enjoyed my doing so, or if he played with me merely out of a sense of parental obligation. It was, in any case, our most effective way of communicating.

My chance to perform in front of an audience

came in my last year of high school. Each winter the Sodality, which organized fund-raising events such as dances and a schoolwide food drive, put on a talent night. My classmate Bob Sweeney, who played bass guitar, invited me to form a trio. We called ourselves the Blue Notes, and our limited repertoire included Elizabeth Cotten's folk classic "Freight Train" and Henry Mancini's jazzy theme from the then-popular television show *Peter Gunn*. It was pretty light stuff, but suited to my limited abilities; Bob wisely denied me a solo. Unlike my father, I didn't place in the competition, but the pulsing beat of "Peter Gunn" brought the house down.

For the Blue Notes, talent night was a one-night stand. It was our last year of high school, and after graduation we drifted apart. I worked that summer in a Montreal office, where I met Nigel, an Englishman who played the clarinet. He introduced me to a weekly jam session that was held in Moose Hall, a large room above a downtown kitchen supply store. There was a full drum set with bass drum, tom-toms, and several cymbals—much more than I had at home—and I eagerly sat in. The music at these jam sessions was Dixieland jazz, with which I was totally unfamiliar, but that didn't stop me; I played.

The following year I began my college studies at McGill University in Montreal. There were more jam sessions, on Saturday afternoons at an off-campus nightclub. I used to go with Bert Kovitz, a hulking clarinetist with whom I worked backstage at the Player's Club, a university theater group to which I belonged. It's a good thing I had practiced to Miles Davis and John Coltrane, for this music was not the watered-down rhythm and blues of the Blue Notes, or the revival Dixieland of Moose Hall. It was the real thing: frenetic bebop. Somehow I kept up. Jam sessions attract musicians of all calibers, who sort themselves out as skill—or, in my case, its lack—becomes evident.

In my third year at McGill, while I was living in a student dorm, I met Hugh Hartwell, a music student who shared my love of jazz. He was a talented pianist, and I sometimes played with him, Sandy Tilley, a bassist and another music student, and Gary Gilmore, a guitarist. Eventually, Hugh found us gigs—paying jobs. I remember a dreadful high school prom, with kids screaming for rock and roll (boring music for a drummer). But mostly we tried to play jazz: a concert in a private boys' school and several nights in a rather louche nightclub that Hugh later gleefully assured me contained a brothel upstairs. That was fitting, since Cole Porter's "Love for Sale" was one of our standards.

I enjoyed playing with Hugh, Sandy, and Gary. Though I was not technically adept and did not take solos, I could play fours—alternating four-bar solos with one of the other musicians. I had more musical intelligence than musical skill, but I had a reasonably good ear, that is, I listened to what the others were doing. I think that's why my friends, who were much more accomplished than I, asked me to play with them. I particularly liked the improvisational nature of the music, which made playing seem more like a conversation than a prepared speech. This conversational quality makes performing jazz intensely private—more so than performing classical music—since the jazz audience is, in a certain sense, listening in rather than listening to. So, playing jazz fit my idea of music.

We also listened. There were many good jazz clubs in Montreal at that time—Casa Loma, Dunn's, The Penthouse, Lindy's, The Black Bottom, and La Tête de Lard (literally, The Fathead). For the price of a drink, and sometimes a modest cover charge, we heard Coltrane, Monk, Mingus, Dizzy Gillespie, Cannonball Adderley, Sonny Stitt, and Wynton Kelly. They were all Americans, but we didn't think of them as foreigners; jazz was an international language.*

We admired these musicians. We didn't just try to play like them, we talked like them, and dressed like them, that is, in three-piece suits, tab-collared shirts,

*The only great Canadian jazz musician at that time was Oscar Peterson, though I don't recall ever hearing him play in Montreal.

and narrow ties. For the only time in my life I wore cuff links, of which I had several pairs, all with matching tie clips. I don't think we noticed that most of the musicians we idolized were black. For one thing, we equally respected many white jazz musicians—Bill Evans, Paul Desmond, Gerry Mulligan—for another, race was hardly as visible an issue in Montreal as it was in most large American cities. I had been in New York City, and camping with my parents in Vermont and New Hampshire, but I had no real experience of American segregation, even though that was the year of the civil rights march on Washington and of Martin Luther King, Jr.'s "I have a dream" speech. Once, when the drummer Max Roach was introducing a set to a largely white audience, I heard a palpable and bitter resentment in his voice—bitter and, to me, inexplicable. After all, I thought naïvely, he was the great Max Roach, what had he to be angry about?*

The following year Hugh and I moved out of the residence and took an apartment on Durocher Street, near the campus. Our roommate was Tony Mawson, an English sociology major who also

*What, indeed! In the 1950s, when the Benny Goodman Quintet appeared on *The Ed Sullivan Show,* Goodman's pianist, the great Teddy Wilson, had been replaced by a white stand-in, for although black performers appeared regularly on Sullivan's television show, blacks and whites could not be shown playing together.

played piano. For the three of us, that school year—1963–64—revolved around jazz, or rather, jazz and girls. My time in a Jesuit boys' school had prepared me for all sorts of things, but not for the mysteries of dating. Being both inexpert and shy, I had experienced little romance during my first two years at college. After I met Hugh and Tony, the pace picked up considerably. They gave me pointers from what seemed to me a vast font of experience. We had parties at the apartment and went to university functions and post-football parties at Hugh's fraternity.

It was Hugh who introduced me to Liz. She was seventeen, in her final year at Trafalgar, a private girls' school. Her father was the president of a large pulp and paper company, headquartered in Montreal. I had never experienced the accoutrements of wealth. It was a heady mix: her family's ample house on the flank of Mount Royal; their summer cottage—larger than my parents' suburban bungalow—on Lake Muskoka in northern Ontario; her stylish friends. I recall leaving to go out on a date and her father casually handing me the keys to his Thunderbird. This at a time when every outing with my father's secondhand Ford Zephyr was preceded—and usually followed—by a cautionary lecture on the hazards of driving. In hindsight, the luxuries that so impressed me were banal, but that made no difference—I was infatuated.

Hugh, Tony, and I fancied ourselves men-about-town. I've never felt as rich as I did that year. Apart from the shared rental of the apartment, which was sparsely furnished, we spent our money only on clothes, food, and drink. (We did have to buy textbooks, but these could always be found secondhand, and resold the following year.) I learned about eating—eating out, that is. Hugh introduced me to steak houses, Tony to roast beef and Yorkshire pudding, both of which were exotic to me. I, in turn, introduced them to goulash (the city had many Hungarian restaurants, run by refugees from the 1956 uprising). We took our dates to downtown bars and to Montreal's many restaurants; the jazz evenings we reserved for ourselves.

Architecture

The Sanctuary of Athena Pronaia in Delphi, July 9, 1964. Sketching is only half about putting pencil to paper; the other half is about careful observation, and looking at buildings became my way of connecting to places.

Although I was consumed by jazz during my first years at McGill, I was not a music student; I was studying to be an architect. I arrived at my vocation more or less by chance. When I was in my last year of high school, it was taken for granted that I would continue on to university. My father never ordered me to in so many words, but he made it clear that knowledge—practical knowledge—had been an important constant in his life, and so it should be in mine. "You can never lose what you know," he used to say. I was a dutiful son, and it would not have occurred to me to disagree. So, while I harbored vague thoughts of indulging a personal interest in history, I accepted that this would not be my future. My college education was to be practical, which meant a profession, but which one? Although I was good at mathematics, my Jesuit education had ill-prepared me for the sciences, nor could I imagine a future as a doctor or lawyer. My father was an engineer, but he rarely discussed his work at home and engineering seemed remote, something dull one did in a factory. I had at least enough wit to recognize that I had an artistic streak, and, rightly or wrongly, I didn't think it would be satisfied by engineering.

I fastened on architecture. To begin with, it was a profession—thus appeasing my parents—and it also promised to accommodate the creativity that I sought. My father's only cousin, Marian, was an architect, which may have influenced me, although he lived in Paris and we had never discussed architecture. I was not one of those children who dreamed early of my future career; while growing up I never paid much attention to buildings. At the age of seventeen, when Le Corbusier was already designing his first houses, I was more interested in—and knew more about—jazz than architecture. Some architects claim to have been inspired by their home environments, but I can't see that the houses I grew up in had much to do with my choice. Our English home in New Malden had been an unremarkable builder house of the early 1900s, whose style, such as it was, was a watered-down version of British Arts and Crafts. Our Canadian home in St. Johns was a one-story bungalow in a new subdivision, with all the banal accoutrements of a fifties ranch house: a low, sloping roof; brick walls with a plywood accent panel near the front door; and a large picture window in the living room.

The bungalow also had a basement, which is where I played with my model train set. I built it on an old Ping-Pong table, constructing the scenery out of plaster of Paris applied over fly screening, just as I had read about in *Railroad Model Craftsman*. The setting of my railroad—the Denver & Rio Grande Western—was the American Southwest, a landscape that I had never seen but that I knew from cowboy movies. The tracks ran through a tunnel (every model train layout has a tunnel), over a balsawood trestle bridge, and beside a water tank that looked like something out of *The Great Train Robbery*. There were several structures—a mine, an engine house, and a general store. I had a little switcher engine, and an assortment of rolling stock, some bought and some homemade, including a cattle car and a red caboose. Since I wasn't very good at soldering, the electrical contacts kept breaking, so the cars mostly stood immobile on sidings. That didn't matter; I was less interested in the operational side of railroading than in building an imaginary miniature world. So, perhaps, my model railroad contained the tiniest hint of my future interest in design and planning.

My chief boyhood experience of architecture was at school. Loyola High School was part of Loyola College, a picture-book quadrangle of Jacobean Revival buildings, built in the 1910s by Frank Peden and Thomas McLaren, two immigrant Scots. The stone-trimmed brick exteriors were decorated with Stuart roses, gargoyles, and other fanciful stone carvings, and the steep tiled roofs were capped by a picturesque assortment of towers, turrets, and cupolas. The college occupied the bulk of the buildings, while the high school was housed in a separate wing; pride of place was given to the chapel, a barn of a building with curved gables and a graceful spire. The classrooms had tall ceilings, polished wood floors, and heavy oak desks, sturdy as carpenters' benches.

I don't think that my splendid surroundings caused me to want to be an architect, but they had a related effect. The five years I spent at Loyola provided me with an experience of architectural beauty that was both unself-conscious and intimate. Later, my Bauhaus education temporarily blinded me to the charms of my Jacobean school, but that initial architectural contact was important. A budding architect needs first to discover that he has a taste for architecture. To become a cook, one must first develop an appreciation for food by eating well—the cooking comes later.

My curriculum at McGill was as much an initiation as an education. To begin with, we—the incoming students—were divested of our preconceptions about architecture. Whatever we knew, or thought we knew, about buildings, based on our everyday surroundings, had to be set aside. Just as army drill sergeants strip trainees down to their fundamentals in order to build them up anew, our teachers made us forget our past experiences and introduced us to an entirely new taste—Bauhaus taste. We were taught that proper buildings had flat roofs, color was to be used sparingly, and decoration was to be avoided altogether. Materials were to be used "honestly," that is, plainly, without extraneous ornament. Unusual building forms were acceptable—indeed, formal invention was praised—but the forms had to be the results of functional and structural requirements, not personal fancy. Although we were expected to study the work of famous contemporary architects, we were roundly criticized if we copied their designs. The idea was that the practical demands of a particular problem would, in some mysterious way, produce attractive buildings. Beauty itself was never mentioned.

I'm not suggesting that my education was narrow-minded—the curriculum was thorough and demanding, combining a sense of idealism with a healthy dose of practicality. We were given a firm grounding in architectural history. We took courses in foundations, steel, reinforced concrete, and surveying in the civil engineering department, and we were expected to know how the buildings that we designed would be constructed. But despite our engineering classes—which, of course, we hated—there was a slight air of unreality about the whole endeavor. We were being taught to make a new kind of architecture—Modern Architecture—but it was one that most of us had never actually seen. Montreal had few examples of Modernist buildings and none that were first-rate. There were many outstanding Edwardian buildings, but these sturdy limestone structures were designed in a variety of historic styles, so they didn't qualify. Montreal's collection of Art Deco buildings from the 1930s is unrivaled in North America, but these buildings weren't modern either, so we ignored them. Instead of experiencing architecture, we studied it by looking at pictures. Thus, the library, rather than the city, became our source of inspiration. The most popular area in the library was the rack of periodicals, where we pored over back issues of *Domus, Architectural*

Forum, and *Architecture d'Aujourd'hui*. These magazines made architecture seem foreign and exotic, which only added to its appeal.

My experience of architecture was not entirely abstract. After graduating from high school, I worked several summers in a small architectural office in Montreal. I started as an office boy but graduated to lettering plans, preparing door and window schedules, and correcting construction drawings. We worked at tilted drafting tables, with T-squares and mechanical pencils. Meadowcroft & Mackay wasn't a glamorous practice, it concerned itself chiefly with industrial buildings, but I was glad of the opportunity. I also learned a lot about architecture, reading blueprints, looking through back issues of architecture magazines in the office library during my lunch break, and talking with Louis Auer, a Viennese architect who befriended me and taught me how to draw.

During my fourth year at McGill, I joined up with Ralph Bergman, a Montrealer, on a team project. We got on well, and enjoyed working together. Ralph told me that he was planning to make an architectural tour of Europe that summer and asked if I would like to join him. Architectural travel is a long-standing tradition that derives from the so-called Grand Tour of the eighteenth and nineteenth centuries, when young British gentlemen traveled the European continent in a sort of educational rite of passage. The typical Grand Tour, focusing on the arts of the Renaissance and antiquity, covered France, Switzerland, Italy, Greece, Germany, and Holland, and could take a year or more. Since Ralph and I had only two months, we followed an abbreviated itinerary. We planned to rent a car in Paris, drive as far as Greece, and return via Italy.

It was Ralph who suggested Greece as a destination. Although I had completed a rigorous history course that included Greek and Roman architecture, and could recite the names and dates of ancient temples by heart, I had no great desire to see the real thing. The temples—that's all the Greeks seemed to build—struck me as repetitive; all those metopes, dentils, and triglyphs. What possible interest could they hold for us now? Our design classes stressed structure and function, which was precisely where the ancient Greeks seemed to be weakest. They didn't even know how to build arches, so they could span only short distances, especially in stone. As for function, unlike the vast Gothic cathedrals, Greek temples were not public gathering spaces, indeed, the enclosure of space seemed almost incidental to their largely symbolic function. But since Ralph was prepared to take the lead in organizing our trip, I bowed to his judgment. In any case, I did want to see Crete; I had read C. W. Ceram's *Gods, Graves and Scholars,* and I wanted to visit the palace of the

Minotaur. I had also recently finished *Zorba the Greek,* which was set in Crete.*

I had another reason to want to go to Europe. The previous year, after Liz graduated, her parents had sent her to Paris "to improve her French." Over the last six months we had maintained a desultory correspondence and, sensing a cooling in her affections, I was anxious to see her. I arrived in Paris a week early and called on her at the rue d'Assas. We took long walks in the nearby Jardin du Luxembourg. Her father, in Paris on business, took us out for dinner at the George Cinq. But for us, at least, the city didn't work her magic. Our romance withered. "All things considered," I recorded drily in my notebook, "it was all very unsatisfactory."

I still had a few days in Paris, which had several examples of buildings by Le Corbusier, a modern architect whose work I badly wanted to see. Of the triad of the so-called pioneers of modern architecture—Walter Gropius, Mies van der Rohe, Le Corbusier—it was Corbu, as we called him, who attracted me the most. I loved his spindly way of drawing, which I imitated, and his spare, uncompromising designs. I had pored over the six volumes of his *Oeuvre complète* and knew that he had designed

*The film, with Anthony Quinn, was released at the end of that year.

two buildings at the Cité Universitaire, a collection of international student residences in a parklike setting in the Fourteenth Arrondissement, so I went there first. The Pavillon Suisse was a student dormitory built by the Swiss government (Le Corbusier was a Swiss native). I recognized it from afar, a little five-story slab with a glass façade. The design was more than thirty years old, but it looked remarkably fresh. Passing under the body of the building, which was lifted off the ground on fat concrete columns, I entered the lobby. I had studied the Pavillon Suisse, but being here was very different from looking at plans in books. Since the *Oeuvre complète* was illustrated in black and white, the colors of the interior walls and ceilings—bright yellow, earth brown, grassy green—were a surprise. So was the curiously shaped lobby: none of the walls were parallel, and some were not even straight. As I walked through the space, everything around me—the randomly spaced columns, the angled walls, a bulging glass partition, and a slightly curved staircase protruding from one side—seemed to shift. It was like being inside a colorful sculpture.

I sat down and sketched, then went next door to the Maison du Brésil. The basic layout was similar—a five-story slab containing the students' rooms, raised up in the air, above the lobby and common room. But the Maison du Brésil was built in 1959, just five years before my visit, and it was an example of Le Corbusier in his so-called brutalist mode. Instead of steel and glass, there was exposed concrete, the uneven marks of the wooden formwork clearly visible; the columns that supported the building were like massive bridge piers; the windows were sheets of plate glass crudely inserted into grooves in the concrete. A curved wall was covered in roughly applied white plaster; the floor, slate laid in a random pattern, was equally rustic. The colors were even more vivid than next door. The overall effect was not modern in any sense I had been taught. On the exterior, the lower block resembled a farmhouse, with fieldstone walls and a sloping roof—a *sloping* roof!

Ralph and I left the city in our tiny Renault, and two days later, in the foothills of the Vosges Mountains near the Swiss border, we stopped to visit what is perhaps Le Corbusier's greatest work, the Chapel of Notre-Dame-du-Haut in Ronchamp. While the buildings that I had seen in Paris had sculptural qualities, the pilgrimage chapel was itself a huge sculpture. "It takes getting used to," I wrote in my notebook. "Only after half an hour I started to really like it. The most startling thing on the exterior is the coarse and rough texture of the plastered walls. The interior is disappointing, at first, because it is so small. Photographs show only parts of the space, and seeing it all at once it seems almost miniature. The contrast between the enormous and scale-less exterior, and the interior, is startling. The three towers are marvelous;

the light streaming over the altar." We stayed two hours, and I made many sketches.

The next day we arrived in Bern, where Ralph, who had done his homework, had the address of Atelier 5, an architectural firm staffed by Corbusier alumni. We met some of the partners, who directed us to a recently completed housing development on the outskirts of the city. Siedlung Halen was the best example of low-rise, high-density housing of the early sixties. I was impressed by the extremely narrow courtyard houses, the sodded roofs, and the compact layout, though slightly put off by the ascetic architecture. "There could be a little more humor in the whole thing," I wrote in my notebook, "although I ought to remember that this is Switzerland." After spending four days in Lausanne touring the Swiss national exposition, we crossed the northeast corner of Italy into Yugoslavia. We descended the Dalmatian coast as far as the old Roman city of Split, where, after visiting Diocletian's palace, we headed inland to Greece.

Our first stop after leaving Thessalonica, a rather dreary city, was the ancient site of Pella, the capital of Alexander the Great. Ralph's *Guide Bleu* highlighted the ruins as an interesting attraction, but the "city" turned out to be an archaeological dig consisting of a few foundations, mosaic floors, and low walls, outlining where houses had once stood. It was rather a letdown. Consequently, I was a little skeptical when Ralph suggested an even longer detour to visit Delphi.

The site of the famous Delphic oracle and sanctuary of Apollo was located on the steep slope of Mount Parnassus, a holy mountain for the ancient Greeks. The first building we came to was the Sanctuary of Athena Pronaia, also known as the Tholos. The unusual temple was circular, about fifty feet in diameter. In fact, the round marble base was pretty much all there was to see. The remains of most of the columns, as well as the wall of the sanctuary, were only a couple of feet high, except for a small fragment that had been reconstructed. More than twenty feet high, three Doric columns were surmounted by a piece of the entablature. I should have been disappointed, but I wasn't. The ancient structure (early fourth century B.C.) had a palpable power, and not only because it was old, and because it was a ruin, but because it was—why did I not expect this?—great architecture.

As I sat sketching, I realized that the photographs of Greek temples that I had studied rarely showed the surrounding landscape, in this case, a dark, looming mountain behind and a spectacular valley stretching out in front. There were a few olive trees nearby, but the mountain slopes were bare. The contrast between the carved marble and the barren hillside—between the man-made and the natural—was extraordinarily moving. The Tholos was so resoundingly vertical that even in its much reduced form it offered a stirring counterpoint to its vast surroundings.

There would be many more such experiences during our Greek tour: the wooded grove at Olympia, the ruins at Mycenae, the great theater at Epidaurus, and the Minoan palace at Knossos—I did get to Crete, after all. And, of course, the Acropolis. If Delphi was a moving overture to my Greek experience, the Acropolis was the resounding climax. I had been taught that ancient Greece was the source of all Western architecture, and walking the rocky height of the Acropolis was like being at the wellspring. The Acropolis had everything: a dramatic site high above the city; a group of temples that had survived the centuries sufficiently intact so that the reconstruction gave the impression of complete buildings rather than fragments; white marble that glowed in the bright sunlight; and the magnificent Parthenon itself. I had studied buildings in books, discussed them with my classmates, and designed projects on paper, but I had never before been so *moved* by a building. I had the same experience as the twenty-four-year-old Le Corbusier, who more than fifty years before had been so overwhelmed by the Parthenon that he called it an "awesome machine."

My architectural tour taught me an important lesson. Because, as a student, I made only drawings and models, I had taken these for the real thing. But architecture was not only about ideas and theories; it had to be experienced. Looking at photographs and drawings was—to continue my culinary analogy—like studying a menu or a recipe instead of eating the meal. In any case, what was good about a building often could not be communicated in pictures, and, conversely, features that seemed dramatic in photographs, often turned out to be only incidental. It was important to know how the Greeks built their temples, how they designed them to create subtle visual effects, and how they conceived of the different parts; but it was not enough. One had to walk among the columns and see the play of sun and shadow on the white marble, and experience buildings as parts of a particular place, whether it was a hill overlooking Athens, or the slope of Mount Parnassus.

I learned something else that summer. I liked looking at buildings. I carried a camera, but mostly I sketched. Sketching is only half about putting pencil to paper; the other half is about careful observation. I couldn't read the road signs in Greece, but I could "read" the buildings, whether they were ancient temples or ordinary village houses. Looking at buildings became my way of connecting to places. In that sense architecture really was—for me, at least—like music. Not what Goethe meant when he called architecture "frozen music," but in the sense that architecture, like music, was an international language. With my background, that made it particularly appealing.

Virtute et Labore

My ambitious student thesis was a hotel in a forest, and resembled a bridge: a high-tech Xanadu.

The early years of an architecture curriculum are devoted to teaching the basics: how to draw, build models, design simple structures. The student learns about building materials, foundations, and functional planning. At some point, these skills and this information have to be combined into a building design. It is a little like swimming: you learn the principles, but at some point you just have to jump in. At first, merely staying afloat is an accomplishment, but quickly you get used to the water, stop flailing around, and start to actually swim. During the fifth year (McGill's was a six-year course), with the basics of architecture under our belts, we were expected to begin to find our own voices. This was the year in which differences in ability, imagination, and talent began to make themselves felt. Architecture is competitive, no less in the classroom than in the real world. There were three of us in the vanguard: Richard Rabnett, a serious, taciturn rugby player from Toronto; Andrejs Skaburskis, a tall Latvian, and, like me, an immigrant; and I. Richard excelled by reason of his sound analysis of problems, and by simply outworking the rest of us. Andrejs, who was a skilled amateur painter, had an artistic streak that manifested itself in powerful graphics. I, capitalizing on my model railroading experience, built intricate models, with stick figures and make-believe trees: a school with a roof that could be lifted off to reveal the individual classrooms; a housing project with an atrium roof of transparent acrylic, scribed to simulate a space frame.

We did not compete for grades, although these were important, especially if you were a scholarship student, as Andrejs and I were; what we valued was one another's esteem and, above all, the favor of our professor. Norbert Schoenauer, our studio master, was generally considered the best design teacher in the school. He had just won a national competition for the Fathers of Confederation Memorial Building on Prince Edward Island, drew beautifully, read widely, and had published a book on courtyard housing. Schoenauer was in his early forties, born in Hungary but educated primarily in Denmark, where he had absorbed a humanist Scandinavian approach to design. He spoke slowly, with a thick accent, but that just gave him more authority. "You should live as if architecture were the most important thing," he used to tell us, "but you should remember that it is not the only thing." He had studied city planning, and he broadened my view of architecture. I learned that while buildings were sometimes sculptural and dramatic—like the Le Corbusier works I had admired the previous summer—they were also places for human activity, and personal aesthetic concerns should never be allowed to override this basic consideration.

Schoenauer introduced us to housing, a field in which he was a recognized expert. It is hard to overstate the position that housing occupied in the field in the mid-1960s; it was not a branch of architecture, it *was* architecture. Housing didn't mean private houses. In all my time at McGill I never designed a house—an individual residence was deemed too trivial, not worthy of an architect's time—but I designed several housing projects. This emphasis reflected the social ideals of the early Modern Movement, which were evident in the work of the younger generation of international architects that we admired: Georges Candilis, Alexis Josic, and Shadrach Woods in France; Alison and Peter Smithson in England; Ralph Erskine in Sweden; Aldo van Eyck in Holland; and, in the United States, Christopher Alexander, whose writing I revered.

The fifth year culminated in the awarding of the CMHC Traveling Scholarship. CMHC stood for Central Mortgage and Housing Corporation, the Canadian federal government's housing agency, which sponsored the award. Each year, the six Canadian schools of architecture chose one student each in the penultimate year, and these students, led by a professor, made a housing tour of North America. Richard, Andrejs, and I knew that one of us would win the scholarship, but since there was no formal application process, and, as far as we knew, it was based not simply on grades but on an overall assessment of our ability and potential, there was little we could do to affect the outcome.

I was fortunate enough to win. In June, the six selected students (representing the universities of British Columbia, Manitoba, Toronto, McGill, Montréal, and Laval) met in Montreal. Our tour leader was Marcel Junius, a professor at the Université de Montréal. He had organized a tour of housing projects in cities in Canada and the United States, as well as visits to several architects' offices and city housing agencies.

Our tour started in Montreal. We drove to Quebec City, where the highlight of the visit—at least for me—was a walk through the picturesque Lower Town. From there we drove to Boston, where we spent most of the day in Cambridge and saw Le Corbusier's new Carpenter Center, which was dramatic although without his characteristic roughness. After stops in Providence and New Haven, we arrived in New York, where we devoted Sunday to art museums and the next day toured apartment buildings by Mies van der Rohe and I. M. Pei. In Philadelphia, we visited Pei's housing in Society Hill, rehabilitated neighborhoods around Washington Square, and the newly built Richards Medical Research Building, by the rising star Louis Kahn. After examining urban renewal in Baltimore, we drove to Washington, D.C., stopping in the new towns of Greenbelt, Maryland, and Reston, Virginia. We saw public housing projects in Pittsburgh and high-rise apartments in Chicago, then flew to San Francisco. A week later we returned to Chicago, where we toured Robert Taylor Homes, which had the reputation of being the largest public housing project in the world—and looked it. We drove to Detroit, where we saw another housing development by Mies van der Rohe (we now understood that Junius was a Mies devotee). Following a brief stop in Toronto, a month to the day after leaving Montreal, we reached Ottawa, where CMHC's headquarters was located.

It was a whirlwind tour, with only a day or two in each city. Barely enough time to form even a first impression. Yet the intensity of the itinerary, with its strong focus on urban housing, left a powerful impression. When it came time to write a report of the trip—something each of us was required to do—I tried to convey something of the frenetic yet concentrated experience. I had just read John Cage's *Silence*, and, influenced by the composer's Zen-like writing style and his gnomic pronouncements, I organized my impressions with one entry per page, some entries long and some very brief. Here are some of my observations:

> *While we were in Boston, we visited a housing project by José Luis Sert, dean of the Harvard school of design. The housing, for Harvard married students, is located in Cambridge. From a distance, we felt that the prominent towers were too strong a symbol for what was, after all, only a student residence, but on seeing the buildings close-up, we realized that pains had been taken to make the project fit into the surrounding brownstone neighborhood. Many of the units were grouped in buildings of three and four stories. There were twenty-four different kinds of apart-*

ments. We asked one of the students who lived there what made her and her husband choose the particular unit they lived in. She answered that though, indeed, there were twenty-four different kinds of units, there was no choice. They simply moved into the first apartment that became available.

During the flight from San Francisco to Chicago, one of our engines broke down, and the additional drag of the stabilizers on one side of the plane caused a great deal of vibration. The stewardess, pale and spilling coffee because of the turbulence, said, "There is nothing to worry about." It turned out she was right.

One day we were sitting in the sun outside the Guggenheim Museum in New York City, getting warm and watching the people on the sidewalk eating ice cream cones. Some of them were sitting on the parapet and, like us, sunning themselves. A fat man in the street with a movie camera was shouting directions at his uncomplaining wife and children. We wondered what it all had to do with the massive, butter-colored colossus behind us. A man sitting on the same bench introduced himself. He was a member of the maintenance crew of the museum, and on his lunch hour. He told us of the Calder mobiles that had recently been exhibited, and about the central dome, whose glass panes expand in the summer and periodically shatter. "It's a bitch of a building," he told us proudly.

Harlem Park, in Baltimore, is a district of about two hundred and fifty acres, with an almost all-Negro population of fourteen thousand. It was once an upper-class white residential neighborhood. Today it is lower-middle-class, or more precisely (though Americans dislike the word) working class. The streets run on a grid defining large blocks. Three-story row houses with stone fronts face the street. Behind the houses, in the inner courts, used to be old slave quarters. After this neighborhood lost its original occupants and assumed the character it has today, the inner blocks deteriorated. The Baltimore Urban Renewal and Housing Agency decided to act. The old slave quarters were pulled down, and the house owners, usually absentee landlords, were required to make repairs in accordance with new health and safety regulations. There remained the question of what to do with the land where the slave quarters had once stood. New buildings would have duplicated the bad conditions that had existed before. It was decided to turn these spaces into inner-block parks, to give the tenants a sense of community. At that point, while the area was by no means a slum, it could hardly be called a strong neighborhood; it had no community organizations, no polit-

ical voice, a growing number of transients, and decreasing social stability. The twenty-five new blocks were formed into the Harlem Park Neighborhood Council. The parks were planned individually, not all at once. The planners met with the block representatives, to discuss their needs. To date, six parks have been built. They cost about $5,000 each, or $1 per square foot. The parks are maintained by the city, though the tenants are responsible for some of the upkeep, such as cutting the grass. As we walked around the parks, which are really play and sitting areas, we saw that some were doing well, and others badly. But this is as it should be. Certain things people must work out for themselves, over time. Visually, the parks are mean and without significance. The old stone houses around them show none of the historic flavor of Georgetown or Society Hill. Yet, these unassuming, even drab, pieces of real estate have helped to make Harlem Park a real community with a stabilizing population, a higher number of homeowners, and a strong voice at City Hall. It seems like a good place to live.

On top of the Art and Architecture Building at Yale there is a tar and gravel roof. There is no handrail or parapet, not even a cant strip. The walls of the building go straight down seventy feet. Around us are the spires and rooftops of the university. There are several chairs on the roof. "What a wonderful way to enjoy the view," I say.

A fact that struck me as we visited various housing projects was the abundance of glass. I don't mean windowpanes—broken glass. It seemed to be everywhere; on the playground, in the corridors, in the street. The children play in it and run through it. I remember a little boy proudly smashing bottles. Wired windows in fire doors in most apartment buildings have been smashed (with baseball bats?). Broken glass is a part of the public housing landscape. Bearing this in mind, we saw a number of schools in Chicago, built as part of housing projects, that were surprising in being almost entirely of glass. And the glass has survived. Children and teenagers seem to be so proud of these concrete and glass creations that they show a respect for them that is lacking towards their own ugly, redbrick "homes."

One afternoon, in Berkeley, the architecture critic Allan Temko told us a story about Louis Kahn. He had invited Kahn, after a party, to see the Christian Scientist church of Bernard Maybeck, the great master of California architecture. The concrete had a magical quality in the moonlight. As they were admiring the church, Kahn, who is not tall, put his hands on the concrete columns and said, "He was a small man, too, wasn't he, Allan?"

On seeing a small house designed by Louis Kahn, I wrote in my sketchbook: "The Beauty of Glass, The Roughness of Concrete, The Scale of Wood."

After visiting Stanford University in California, we decided to drive back to the city along the Pacific coast. Between us and the coast highway lay a ridge of mountains. The road map showed a straight line running across these mountains and joining the highway, which continued to San Francisco. We followed this road up into the hills, where it turned into a gravel track. The road that had seemed so inoffensive on the map took on evil proportions. As we rose higher, the mist grew too thick to be able to see more than twenty feet ahead. Occasionally, we glimpsed the lush slopes below. When we finally drove out of the mountains and out of the fog, the Pacific Ocean seemed almost an anticlimax.

Found written on the wall of a studio in the school of architecture of the University of Pennsylvania: KAHNFUSED.

We visited Mill Creek, a public housing project in Philadelphia designed by Louis Kahn. There were two high-rise towers with large balconies. The balconies had no handrails, instead they were screened from top to bottom with what appeared to be chain-link fencing. Whether or not Mr. Kahn designed them in this way I don't know. There was an immediate outburst from our group, upon seeing children playing in these veritable cages. Our middle-class sensibilities were offended. But if they were my children on the thirteenth floor, would I have settled for anything less?

There are two Americas, one black and one white. When we walked through the Negro districts of Philadelphia, we could have been in another city. This feeling became more and more frequent. It could sometimes be exotic, the same way that American jazz could be exotic, but more often it wasn't. It was a characteristic of the American city that was largely ignored, and beside it our talk of traffic segregation and urban redevelopment sounded shallow. In this regard, the large energy that was being spent on urban renewal (Beacon Hill, Georgetown, Society Hill), seems misdirected or, at least, overemphasized. Façade architecture and modish revival is a fad that does not address the real problem of cities: that of the "greater number."

In the back alleys of Quebec's Lower Town, the children were playing ball. It was just beginning to rain, and they were gathered under a gallery, keeping dry and playing just the same. It was dark and moody in the alley. There was no grass, and little sun, but, on the other hand, there were no cars either. Farther along, a boy in a red T-shirt swung from a fire escape.

The CMHC scholarship consisted of two parts; following the monthlong tour, we were required to spend eight weeks working as interns at the corporation's headquarters in Ottawa. That meant we had to find a place to live. Thanks to our tour, we had become convinced that public housing was the most urgent problem facing architects, and we thought that we—all solidly middle-class—would learn something if we could actually live in a public housing project. But when we proposed the idea to our hosts, they soundly rejected it as impractical. A few days later, we were officially welcomed to the corporation by its vice president, Jean Lupien. When he asked us how we were doing, we said fine, but . . . and cheekily reiterated the public housing suggestion. "What a good idea," he said and instructed his assistant to take care of the details.

The six of us moved into a three-bedroom apartment in a low-rise block of Mann Avenue Apartments, a public housing project in Ottawa. The neatly maintained buildings and trimmed lawns were nothing like the broken-glass places that we had seen during our American tour. In fact, our accommodations were similar to the apartment I had lived in when my family first moved to St. Johns. I'm not sure exactly what we students gained by the experience, but it was fun to live together. My roommate was Bing Thom, from the University of British Columbia. He had grown up in Vancouver, but he, too, was an immigrant—born in Hong Kong. Bing was short, with a shock of black hair and the nimblest mind I had ever encountered. He was also an imaginative designer. To keep our room ventilated during the hot weather, we had to keep the door open, which encouraged our colleagues to drop in while we were trying to work. Bing bought several boxes of steel washers and made a beaded curtain. He explained that, while the strands allowed the air to pass through, the washers were so heavy that they discouraged casual visitors—but without making us appear antisocial.

On weekdays, we bicycled to CMHC, which was housed in a sprawling office building on Montreal Road. The majority of the employees seemed to be accountants administering home-mortgage programs, but there was a small architecture and planning division that oversaw the construction of federally funded public housing projects across the country. That was where we were based. Our internship consisted of reading research reports, studying old housing projects, and attending talks by various housing officials. We soon got bored—we fancied ourselves designers and we wanted to design—so we complained. We must have appeared an insufferable group of malcontents to David Crinion, the chief architect, but he humored us. The corporation was building a public housing project in Winnipeg, Manitoba, and he handed us the program documents and background information, and told us to get to work. To make things more realistic, we would present our designs, as they evolved, to him and his staff. At the same time, we could sit in on the presentations of the actual project by its Winnipeg architects.

It was like a school assignment, except without the distractions of other courses, and with the added benefit of informed criticism from experienced professionals. Bing and I formed a team. The program called for a large number of units, which would normally have required multistory apartment buildings. As a result of our tour, we were convinced that high-rise living was a bad solution for poor families, and we devised an extremely dense arrangement of interlocking houses that gave each household its own front door and private yard. Collaborating proved awkward at first, since whatever Bing sketched seemed to be built of Western red cedar, while my designs always looked like heavy concrete. We compromised on brick.

During those two months at Mann Avenue Apartments, Bing and I became fast friends. When we weren't working on our project, we talked—about architecture, housing, planning, and especially about our theses. The final-year thesis, a traditional part of the architectural curriculum, was not an academic dissertation but a building project—of the student's own choosing. The project did not have to be large, but it was expected to be exploratory, and it was supposed to demonstrate the full range of a student's abilities in analysis, programming, design, and construction. In short, the thesis was the capstone of our university education.

I had chosen tourism as my topic. "Tourism is essentially a geographical experience," I wrote in my notebook, "a free and leisurely method of learning about the world and about ourselves and our ways of life." Which was a pretty fair description of the trip I had taken with Ralph the previous summer. I wasn't yet sure what sort of tourist facility I was going to design, but I did have a general location. A friend had told me about the Gaspé, a peninsula near the mouth of the St. Lawrence, six hundred miles east of Montreal. The most famous geographic feature of this remote area is Percé Rock, a massive piece of limestone off the tip of the peninsula, pierced—*percé*—by an unusual fifty-foot-high natural arch. Just before I left on the CMHC tour, I had driven the Gaspé coastal road. It was early spring, and there were no other visitors. I was immediately taken by the evocative landscape of tall cliffs, steeply rising inland mountains, big skies, and empty stretches of strand along the sparkling waters of the Gulf of St. Lawrence. It was as beautiful as I had been told.

It might appear strange that, interested as I was in public housing and urban problems, I should have chosen this topic. I might rather have followed the example of Moshe Safdie, who had represented McGill on the scholarship tour five years earlier (I found his report in the CMHC library). He turned his experience into a legendary housing thesis that was actually being built for the upcoming Montreal world's fair. But I didn't take Safdie's lead. Maybe it was the moving experience of the Greek temples that made me want to design something in the natural landscape. Or perhaps it was simply the arrogance of youth, which feels itself able to do anything. After several months of thinking about the problem of public housing, I wanted to try something totally different.

I spent a lot of my free time in the CMHC library that summer, taking out books on tourism, recreation, human geography, and ecology. I read about the history and economy of the Gaspé, which had been a tourist attraction since the nineteenth century, despite its remoteness and the shortness of its summers. I found reports about building in wilderness areas and unearthed a government study of wood plastics, which I thought might make a good building material, since the Gaspé was rich in timber. I came across a FORTRAN planning program written by Christopher Alexander and compiled a list of forty-five separate design requirements, which I laboriously transferred to punch cards. That fall, back at the university, Richard Rabnett and I tried to run the program on the engineering faculty's computer—without success. I also collected background information about innovative architectural projects dealing with tourism: a regional recreation master plan in Languedoc; a Club Med in Israel; a facility in Lake Balaton, Hungary; capsulelike skiers' cabins in Japan; and a northern resort in Finland. In short, following Norbert Schoenauer's teaching, I approached my problem from the broadest possible perspective.

During my tour of the Gaspé, I had noted a potential building site for my thesis not far from Percé, on one of the few protected bays along that craggy coastline. My first design sketches showed a sort of nomadic camp consisting of prefabricated shelters. But I soon became dissatisfied with the scale of such a project—I wanted something bigger. I decided to take a more visionary approach. If visitors arrived by plane instead of by car, I could plan a much larger facility. And it might be more challenging if the site were inland instead of on the coast. The map showed a small lake, which I thought would make an interesting location, but it was twelve miles from the putative landing strip. No problem, I could simply build an aerial cable car line joining the two; it was more dramatic arriving that way, anyway. I found this freewheeling problem solving to be a lot more fun—and easier—than analyzing forty-five design requirements, and my project grew more and more outlandish. Since visitors were flying in, there was no reason that the resort could not operate year-round (instead of only during the short Gaspé season of two months). But how would people get around in the harsh winter weather? I didn't like the idea of glassed-in walkways, but what about tunnels? Since the distances were long, I added moving sidewalks. The final extravagances of my high-tech Xanadu were the hotel rooms themselves. I wanted the visitors to experience dramatic views, but the problem with building in a dense forest was that you couldn't see very far. A high-rise building struck me as banal, and I didn't want to chop down a lot of trees. My solution was to suspend the rooms from an arched structure that spanned the valley like a huge bridge. Now guests had an unimpeded view, down the valley to the St. Lawrence below. Since there were two valleys leading to the lake, it was just as easy to have two bridge buildings as one.

My thesis, which had started as a modest tourist village, had grown into an architectural complex of monumental proportions. But when it came time to prepare the final drawings and models, I got cold feet. Bing and I had discussed the idea that a thesis ought to emphasize the design process rather than final product. Perhaps wanting to downplay what, even to me, must have appeared a far-fetched project,

I decided to document the evolution of my design—in excruciating detail. I included my background research, photos of study models, and sketches of discarded alternatives. The information was recorded on eight-and-a-half-by-eleven-inch sheets, without color or fancy graphics. The final design was likewise depicted on small, diagrammatic drawings, with Corbusian insouciance. I allowed myself one theatrical gesture. The model maker in me couldn't resist building a large model of the site, with a glass lake and several thousand pine trees made out of tiny pieces of green sponge.

The grand finale to a thesis was the "crit," when students presented their finished projects to a panel of critics—professors and visiting architects. Crits could be intimidating since they tended to take their own course, depending on the tenor of the questions and answers, and the unpredictable mood of the critics. A crit could be a lovefest—or a feeding frenzy. A critic might praise some picayune detail, encouraging other plaudits and leading to unanimous commendation. Conversely, someone might discover a tiny unresolved flaw, producing further scrutiny, revealing more defects, and pretty soon the scheme would be on the floor in tatters. As my own review unfolded, it became clear that the critics were not impressed by either my implausible project or my quixotic attempt to document its evolution. Schoenauer remained silent—never a good sign. A visiting architect expressed skepticism about the structural logic of the arches. Someone else questioned the wisdom of building in such a remote area. I answered as best I could, but I could see from the frowns that the seeds of doubt had been planted.

When the final grades and awards were posted, Richard, who had designed a sensible harbor-front housing scheme, topped the list, with a prestigious traveling scholarship; my friend Ralph, who had not previously been a standout, garnered second place with a beautiful little conference center; and Andrejs, who had designed a complicated mixed-use downtown project, won the other traveling scholarship. My name was farther down the list, although I did receive a medal. It was inscribed "Virtute et Labore." I thought it a consolation prize—and at that point I desperately needed consoling—but in truth it was more than I deserved.

Part III

My first commission, a house on Formentera. Once I came to terms with the fact that my design didn't have to be "different," that I didn't have to try so hard to be the next Le Corbusier, the rest was easy.

Formentera Spring

May 1967. The Balearic Islands were a whistle-stop on the alternative Grand Tour: Haight-Ashbury–Ibiza–Kathmandu–Bali. My friends Jibus and Nicolle on a carefree afternoon.

After graduating, I worked for eight months in several architectural offices, saving money to go back to Europe. The tour with Ralph had whetted my appetite, but this time I planned a leisurely trip of a year or more. If I had been honest with myself—which I wasn't—I would have admitted that travel was also a chance to escape. Not merely from the tedium of daily routine but also from the weight of responsibility. During my last year and a half at university, I had fallen in love. I met Claudia at a party at a friend's apartment. A freshman, she was small, serious, and lovely. It was what the French call a *coup de foudre*, a lightning strike—for both of us. Whatever time I had away from my schoolwork I spent with her (my jazz evenings had become things of the past); she even went with me on my magical tour of the Gaspé. Some couples might have married after graduation—as my younger brother would do—but we didn't. There was indecision on her part, a lack of urgency on mine. We didn't break up, exactly, but it was understood that I was under no obligation to return quickly, and that she was under none to wait for me. I sensed that she was uncertain, but I took her hesitation as an excuse to get away—at least for a while. Also, the less than stellar culmination of my thesis still rankled, and travel seemed like a good way to put that episode behind me. If I couldn't win a traveling scholarship, I would provide my own.

I booked passage on a German freighter. It was cheaper than flying and seemed like a fitting way to begin my *Wanderjahr*. I boarded the ship in Quebec City and sailed through the broad gulf of the St. Lawrence River into the Atlantic. It was January, and the open ocean was rough. I developed a queasy stomach from the ship's motion, which made it difficult to face the hearty dumplings and fried *Wurst* that were the standard fare of the crew. When I did feel better, I discovered another liability of sailing on a foreign ship: the captain and his crew didn't speak English. Since I was the only passenger, I had no one to talk to and spent most of the crossing in my cabin reading. It wasn't until the last day that I met one of the seamen, Maciek Zochowski, a Pole. He persuaded me that, if I wanted to travel around Europe, I should buy a car in Germany, since German cars carried a hefty tax, based on the engine size, but were tax-free if they were for export. After we docked in Hamburg, he helped me find a seven-year-old Volkswagen—my first car—for three hundred dollars. I was off.

My first stop was Leiden, where Ankie, a Dutch girl I had met in Crete two years before, was studying. During my relationship with Claudia, I had continued to correspond with Ankie, although she seemed surprised when I turned up. We spoke vaguely of traveling to North Africa together. Could I wait a month until she finished her courses? she asked. I drove to Paris, where I stayed with my uncle Marian and his wife, went sightseeing, took a ceramics course, and attended a class on French civilization at the Sorbonne.

Before the month was up, my travel plans changed. Ankie was no longer sure she wanted to travel—or, at least, to travel with me. I think we both breathed a sigh of relief. Since there was nothing holding me back, I set off immediately, but with another traveling companion. Ed Satterthwaite was an architect from Philadelphia whom I had met in Montreal—we worked together in Moshe Safdie's office on Habitat, the housing thesis that was now the centerpiece of the world's fair. Ed was several years older than I, a talented draftsman and brimming with architectural ideas. We spent many of our evenings after work in a downtown bistro, which was where the idea of going to Europe had taken birth. Ed was obsessed by building with mass-produced geometrical elements—blending Frank Lloyd Wright with Buckminster Fuller—and wanted to find a congenial Greek island where he could spend a few months putting his ideas down on paper. We had traveled to Europe separately, but when we met up in Paris, we decided to continue together. I liked the idea of going back to Greece, but I wanted to see Spain first. Just as Kazantzakis had drawn me to Greece, another writer attracted me to Spain. In my last year of high school, I had discovered Hemingway, read all his novels and stories, including *Death in the Afternoon,* and I was set on attending a *corrida.* It turned out that Ed was a Hemingway devotee, too—with his prematurely grizzled beard he even looked a little like the writer—so we agreed on Spain. I had a vague plan to sell my car once we got there, and either travel to Greece or return to Paris to find work in an architect's office.

Stopping at Versailles and Chartres, we drove down the Loire valley, visiting each château in turn. It was midwinter, and there were few tourists; on the other hand, the great stone structures were bitterly cold, as were the youth hostels in which we slept. In Sarlat, a fourteenth-century village high in the mountains of Dordogne, we spent the night feeding a fire with wood scraps, trying to warm a damp, drafty room. There were three of us—we had met Agathe, a Parisian painter, who had a show in Sarlat. She invited us to her parents' summer house in nearby Montferrier, where we spent the next night. Here, with apologies to Papa and Dylan Thomas, are the notes made the following day by a wide-eyed twenty-three-year-old:

> *We had an evening meal that was the best I have had in many days. Duck pâté with bread, macaroni and eggs, cheese, fruit, and the local wine, white, a little sweet, and cut with water. And later that night, crepes with jam and sugar, baked apples, and tea. We visited a neighboring farmer to get fresh milk and saw the simple way in which they (mother, father, two children, and grandparents) lived, and how hard they worked. And we passed the old crumbled ivy-grown-covered-over house of mad Bill, who lives with his animals. And sat on stumps and*

watched the sun set. And ate chestnuts roasted over the fire. And cut wood and marveled how quickly it burned, and took photographs of the ravaged table covered with scraps of the fine meal and hoped that it would keep the memory of it alive. And rubbed smoke out of our eyes, and each had a theory of how best to make the fire, and felt drowsy by its warmth, and awoke to silence, and saw the mist so low over the valley you could not see across (as you could the evening before, across far across, and beyond that), and drank the milk fresh from the night before, fresh from between the farmer's fingers, and started a fire, and sat, and slowly got into the new day, like a girl you just met and are not sure of.

—February 27

Making a detour to drop Agathe off in Périgueux, we descended the Massif Central, stopping in Albi, the birthplace of Toulouse-Lautrec, to see the spectacular cathedral and continuing to the medieval town of Carcassonne—famous among architects for its restored fortifications. As we went south, the weather turned warmer, so by the time we crossed the Pyrenees into Spain it felt like Florida. It was March 1, my birthday. Having had our fill of architectural sightseeing, we bypassed Barcelona and Gaudí and drove to the coastal resort town of Sitges—empty at this time of year—where we rented a small house, a cabin, really, facing the bay. Ed spent the mornings filling his notebook with intricate architectural sketches, so I felt obliged to work, too. I sketched: buildings in the town, fishermen mending their nets, our tiny kitchen, a cat that came with the house. We passed the afternoons drinking wine at a local waterfront bar, which was owned by the improbably named Manuel Ferrer Hill, who resembled John Wayne. We practiced our Spanish on his pretty daughter, Carmen. I jotted this poem in my notebook:

I hear the sea
Pouring mournfully up the beach,
And crashing the worn rocks.
And I hear
Carmen brushing the equally worn stoop of her
father's café.
And really, I hear nothing else,
Only sometimes the scratch-scratching of my pen.
—March 15

After two weeks we left Sitges and drove to Valencia for Las Fallas, a weeklong, citywide festival of fireworks, parades, displays, pantomimes, and bullfights. I loved the somber drama and pageantry of the bullfights, and also the eating and drinking, the twice-daily fireworks (*fallas* means "fires"), and the excited crowd. After attending the last *corrida*, which included the famous matador Antonio

Ordoñez, Ed and I decided to split up. He was impatient to get to Greece before his funds ran out, while I wanted to see a bit more of Spain. We talked vaguely of meeting in Mykonos, but, in truth, I think that after a month together, we were looking forward to traveling alone.

I had a vague plan to return to Paris, perhaps to find a job. But first I thought I would take a look at the Balearic Islands, one of which—Ibiza—was less than a hundred miles offshore. I had seen its traditional white architecture illustrated in magazines, and the place seemed worth a visit. I drove to Cullera, the port of Valencia, and parked the Volkswagen on the busy main street, near the quay where the overnight Ibiza ferry berthed.

I arrived in Ibiza early the next morning. The tall stucco houses surrounding the harbor were attractive, but although it was only March—hardly the height of the tourist season—the steep, narrow streets were already teeming with visitors. The town, founded by Carthaginians and subsequently invaded by Romans, Normans, Arab pirates, and Catalans, was now firmly in the grip of throngs of German tourists from the cruise ships anchored offshore. The crowded, agitated atmosphere didn't appeal to me, and I decided my impulsive detour had been a mistake. But since the Valencia ferry didn't sail until that evening, I had the rest of the day to kill.

As I wandered through the harbor, looking at the yachts and motorboats, I caught sight of a tall, striking girl. She wore loose, patterned clothing and, carrying a straw bag, strode purposefully along the stone pier, her long, fair hair streaming behind her. Definitely not Spanish—perhaps Swedish or Californian—she had the aplomb of beautiful women everywhere.

At the end of the pier, the girl boarded a large motor launch. A battered, hand-painted sign attached to the handrail read "M/N Joven Dolores, Ibiza–Formentera, 17 pesetas." The launch was apparently sailing to somewhere called Formentera—which couldn't be far since it cost about thirty cents. I was too shy to approach the beautiful girl, but the rusty *Joven Dolores* appealed to me—it was exactly the sort of boat tourists would avoid. I had all my belongings in a canvas bag, so I jumped aboard. In short order, the launch headed out of the harbor and turned toward the low, gray headland of a small island in the distance.

Forty-five minutes later, we docked at a rather forlorn wharf. This was no picturesque Mediterranean port; in fact, there were no buildings at all. The few people who disembarked simply walked off down the road, the beautiful blonde, whom I never saw again, was one of them. I thought I would look for a village where I could get something to eat. I couldn't see any buses or taxis, or even any cars.

After buying a soft drink from the roadside stall, I set off.

I walked for half an hour. The island was flat and extremely rocky; the sole vegetation seemed to be cacti, and the occasional olive grove. There were stone walls everywhere, and many isolated farmhouses, but nothing that looked like a village. (Actually, the main village of the island was nearby, but I had taken a wrong turn.) The road was dusty, the March sun unexpectedly hot, and I was hungry, tired, and becoming dispirited. My adventurous mood of the morning was flagging.

I was sitting dejectedly on a stone wall when two people, who must have been on the launch, caught up with me. We exchanged hellos. The man, tall and dark-haired, introduced himself as Michel Mendès France. I recognized the famous French surname and later learned he was the ex–prime minister's son. His friend was Maryvonne. They were Parisian graduate students—mathematicians—on a hitchhiking holiday in Spain. I spoke halting French, and perhaps because of the shared language (French is particularly suited to socializing), or simply through politeness, they invited me to join them. We spent the day on the beach and, in the late afternoon, went to a bar called Fonda Pepe in the village of San Fernando, where Michel was to meet some friends who had rented a house on the island.

His friends arrived. It turned out that, although

they had reserved a house for a month, their plans had changed. They needed to find someone to rent it—perhaps I would be interested? they asked. Perhaps, I said. We went to look at the house. It was a solid-appearing stone structure with a clay-tile roof. The accommodations were spartan: no running water (only a rainwater cistern), no electricity, candles and a kerosene lamp for light, a kerosene burner to cook on, an outdoor privy. There was a small shuttered window—no glass—in each of the two bedrooms; the third room, which stretched across the front of the house, had no windows at all, only a large wooden door. The floor was bare rock with the cracks cemented over; the ceiling was the underside of the roof tiles. There was very little furniture: several Lilliputian chairs, a couple of benches that did double duty as tables, and two wooden bedsteads. Roughly plastered walls, devoid of adornment, completed the severe decor. To some people, the house might have appeared bare, but to a young architect weaned on Le Corbusier's Mediterranean architecture, it was perfect. I had never been attracted by the picture-postcard prettiness of Italian hillside towns and Aegean island villages, but the plain stone houses of this plain stony island were different. They had the spare and unsentimental quality of Hemingway's best writing, which was one of the things that had brought me to Spain in the first place.

By that evening I was a householder, or at least a

tenant. I invited Michel and Maryvonne to stay with me—it seemed the least I could do—which they did for two days before returning to the mainland. It was only after seeing them off at the dock that I had a brief moment of panic. What was I doing in this desolate place?

I am sitting in the evening; it is about two hours since sunset and I have finished eating and have just made a cup of coffee. In the fireplace the log that has not caught fire sizzles and crackles. In front of me, on the bench, the kerosene lamp makes a noise, which stops after I adjust it. I can hear the wind blowing outside. It has been blowing all day like that, and I expect it will continue to do so for a few days more. There is a candle burning, in the niche in the wall, and it casts shadows, particularly inside the niche, which was made for water jugs and has a board with three holes for the jugs to sit in. I use it for my shaving things and there is also a rusty can with flowers in it standing on the part between the holes. In the niche there is a coffee grinder, and a mirror which I bought for fourteen pesetas in the dry goods store in San Francisco. It had a flower pattern painted on but I scratched it off with my penknife and now it is a good mirror. Every second morning I hang it on a nail, outside, while I shave.

—April 6

Thanks to Michel, I fell in with a group of vacationing Parisians. Although I had studied French in high school, I'd used it rarely, but all those years of memorizing vocabulary and declining irregular verbs paid off, and I was soon fluent. I made an unremarkable discovery: the best way to learn to speak a language is to want to say something. Michel's friends introduced me not only to the pleasure of the language but also to Gallic manners, old-fashioned formality with hand shaking, conviviality, and the delightful rituals of eating.

I was used to English-speaking people being tongue-tied by my name—something to do with the lack of vowels—and often making some sort of lame joke. No wonder Korzeniowski changed his name to Conrad. But, perhaps because Paris has been home to so many Polish and Russian émigrés over the centuries, my French friends seemed entirely unfazed by my name. They even pronounced my Christian name correctly—*Vee-told.* But the strangest thing, for me, was that they considered me not *canadien* but *polonais.* In Canada, I was an immigrant from somewhere else; in Europe, with its ancient history of cultural and ethnic divisions, everyone belonged to a place; I was a Pole. It was a novel feeling.

It turned out that Formentera was hardly as desolate as it had first appeared. There were many expatriates, a globe-trotting assortment of what were starting to be called hippies; Americans and English, mostly, with a few Germans and Scandinavians. They gave themselves exotic names—Captain Billy, Watahamee John, Dutch Tom—and wore colorful clothes and beads. They had no visible means of support, although it was rumored that one was a bullion smuggler, and several others were obviously drug dealers. The usually conservative Spanish authorities (this was still the Franco era) tolerated odd behavior on this remote island, and since there was no electricity or running water, there were no hotels and no tourists. This, together with cheap accommodations, made the Balearic island a whistle-stop on the alternative Grand Tour: Haight-Ashbury–Formentera–Kathmandu–Bali.

The hippies were friendly, and fun to party with, although their blithe indolence could be wearying. One evening at Fonda Pepe I struck up a conversation with a newcomer, a small Englishman named Mike Shaw. He was a painter from the Isle of Wight who had just spent a year in the Australian outback. Mike's London gallery periodically sent him small sums of money in exchange for completed canvases, so he was anxious to start working, as soon as he found a house to rent on the island. I invited him to stay with me, and we spent the next three days looking for a house. We came across a double house and almost rented it together but finally decided that solitude was better for working.

For I had a project of my own. One of my new French friends, Jacques Renaud, a Parisian sculptor, owned a plot of land on the island and had asked me if I would design a small house for him. Jacques was on holiday, and before he returned to Paris, we agreed. My first commission! Although I had never designed a house as a student project, I didn't think it would be difficult. I quickly set to work. The site, like most of the island, was treeless, bare rock. I started sketching a series of long, low stone walls that could enclose rooms, shaded terraces, and protected courtyards.

Mike's house was on the other side of the island, and we visited each other every few days. The next time he came, I proudly showed him my sketches. His reaction surprised me. He pointed out that my design didn't look much like the other houses on Formentera. Of course it doesn't, I said huffily, it's modern, it's supposed to look different. But why can't it be the same? he insisted.

I had been taught in school that an architect should always be original—different—so I didn't have a good answer to Mike's question. But it nagged at me. After three weeks on the island, my first impression of its architecture had, if anything, intensified: the plain stone houses suited this arid, weather-beaten place, and I knew from personal experience that their cool, dark interiors suited the climate. So, maybe I should look more closely at the architecture around me. I stopped designing and started sketching, first my own house, then those of friends and acquaintances, as well as abandoned ruins. I bought a tape measure. Perhaps by making detailed drawings—what architects call measured drawings—I could uncover the secrets of these houses. How high was that comfortable ledge? What was the width of that cozy niche? The size of that window? My project also gave me the opportunity to meet the local people, who generally kept to themselves. In my rudimentary Spanish, I asked about the histories of specific houses. I learned that my house was called C'an Pep Ferrer and had been built in 1884, when the island was resettled after one of its frequent and devastating droughts. That made it relatively new, for the older houses dated back to the sixteenth century. At that time the island was subject to raids by Algerian pirates, and some of the structures I measured resembled little fortresses, with tiny windows that were really loopholes. I also learned about traditional building techniques, such as using layers of seaweed from the beach to insulate the roof, and building walls out of two types of stone, a harder stone facing the sun and a softer stone on the shady side. It was enjoyable work, tramping around the island, sketching and measuring, then drafting detailed plans at home.

How to build a cistern. First of all you must know why. The water table is at least 100 feet down, it is often saline, and the 100 feet are solid rock. However, because the ground is rocky, rainwater is not absorbed immediately. So you find the lowest point in a rocky area and dig a cistern. When it rains, the captured water pours into the cistern and eventually fills it up. (If you have no sloping rocky area near your house, you can construct one using flat stones and cement.) Most of the cisterns are about twenty cubic meters, so digging is quite a job. You use a kind of pick. It usually takes a few months. I met an old fellow of sixty-five who was digging his second cistern by hand, because he wanted to grow more flowers.

—May 19

It was a beautiful spring, with red poppies growing along the footpaths; warm days and balmy nights. When my monthlong lease expired, I found another house to rent. C'an Moli—whose name derived from the massive stone windmill that stood nearby—was newer, and lacked the primitive character of my previous home. There were two bedrooms, a wide center hall that served as a living room, and an extra room that I used as a studio. The south-facing porch was surrounded by cacti. I could afford to stay here a long time, for life in Formentera was inexpensive: a shot of brandy in the Fonda Pepe was ten cents; a liter of wine, fourteen cents; the best meal in the island's sole restaurant, one dollar. Mostly I ate at home. "Do you remember the story of how peasants cook in a big pot, adding something every day?" I wrote in a letter home. "Well, that is just how I'm cooking. Beans, carrots, onions, peppers, meat sometimes, potatoes, corn, peas, tomatoes are all inside so far. It is a good way to eat, especially here, where fresh vegetables are expensive and some days nonexistent, and all meat is imported, and must be cooked right away because in the heat nothing keeps." To reassure my parents, I added: "I am eating well, outside all day, and walking a lot, in other words, as healthy as can be. Also very brown from working in the sun. Don't worry."

Periodically I took the launch to Ibiza, where I bought fresh vegetables and art supplies, ate a restaurant meal, and dropped in to a bookstore that sold the London *Times* and English-language paperbacks. I was reading Camus, Koestler, and Orwell, which shows my relentlessly introspective frame of mind. I carried a sketchbook with me when I left the house and filled it with drawings: old ladies in the town square, goats, an empty village street, an Ibiza café, and an inexplicably large number of delicately colored drawings of spring flowers. And sketches of girls—many girls.

The young girls hold cigarettes.
Wind blowing smoke before their faces
And ash across their innocence.

Brown legs brown,
The down glitters in the light.
The sight of so much flesh
Makes the desire crawl into my bones.
—May 11

"The fact that I am alone bothers me less than I would expect," I wrote in my journal, "and I am getting used to it." Brave words, but not exactly true, judging from my yearnful poems. I was hardly a recluse. I saw Mike regularly, dropped in on Sioma Baram, another painter whom I had met through Jacques, and had a wide circle of acquaintances. My classmate Andrejs Skaburskis, who was touring Europe, visited for two weeks. But I missed female company. It would have been wiser to find a companion *before* retreating, as my grandfather had done. I had a brief affair with a willful French woman, pined for Lorence, a winsome hippie, and wrote long letters to Claudia in Montreal. At one point it appeared that she might come, although, much to my disappointment, the visit never materialized.

So I lost myself in my work. I amassed a lot of information about the old houses of Formentera, and I now understood how completely out of place a modern house would look here. Although the Formentera houses did have flat roofs, their tiny windows made them look Moorish rather than Modern—Arabs had occupied the island for several hundred years during the Middle Ages. The buildings on the island spanned several hundred years, but their consistency was striking, as if the builders were content to use and reuse the same architectural vocabulary—though not necessarily to say the same thing, for no two houses were identical.

But I wasn't any closer to a design. I could have simply modified one of the traditional houses I studied, but everything in my training went against this commonsense expedient. It had to be *my* design. This was a problem, and at one point I panicked; I couldn't sleep, I got headaches and broke out in a rash. I had spent six years studying how to be an architect, and here at my first opportunity, my imagination was failing me! Finally, slowly, I worked my way out of my predicament. A distinctive feature of the traditional, flat-roofed houses was that large rooms typically had taller ceilings than small rooms, and the differences were clearly visible on the exterior. I decided that each of the rooms in my house should have a different ceiling height, making a composition of different-size boxes. I also made an important discovery about materials. The stone walls of the traditional houses on the island were either left bare or plastered and painted white. It occurred to me that Jacques's house could have both; the variety would be more interesting to look at, and it would make the house appear as if it had been built at different times. This aperçu doesn't sound like much, but it took me six weeks to figure it out. For someone trained in "form follows function," it was a major breakthrough.

Once I had come to terms with the fact that my design didn't have to be "different," that I didn't have to try so hard to be the next Corbu—one of the problems with my thesis—the rest was easy. I simply had to take all that I had learned about dimensions and proportions, sun and shade, and niches and dark interiors, and apply it to the problem at hand, which, in truth, was not really that complicated. The small house needed only two rooms and a kitchen. One room would be low, the other slightly higher and include a sleeping loft; the kitchen would be raised several feet more to provide a view of the distant sea to the south (the space below the floor serving as an aboveground cistern). I built a cardboard model, took it outside, and studied the effects of the sun at different times of day, arranging the three rooms so as to create a protected, walled courtyard. On the east side, I placed a terrace with poles and wires for growing vines, where you could eat breakfast. An outside stair led to a roof terrace, which could be used for sleeping on warm nights. The two rooms, which had no specific functions—they could be used for sleeping, eating, or socializing—were dark, with low windows that were invisible from a distance. The kitchen was bright. From a distance, its two square windows would look like a pair of eyes.

* * *

My journal from that period includes a quote from Albert Einstein—copied from a newspaper. "To understand the world one must not be worrying about oneself." That was a problem with my *Wanderjahr*. When I was studying the Formentera houses, working on the house, or sketching, I became lost in my subject, but I spent too much time precisely worrying about myself. In the process, I discovered an uncomfortable truth. I had always worked hard to impress my parents, my teachers, my classmates. Cut adrift from this comfortable meritocracy—comfortable, that is, if you were willing to play by the rules—I was not sure what I was supposed to do. For example, I had no inkling of how one went about starting an architectural career—that was one subject no one had taught me. I imagined that commissions would just magically fall into my lap. Well, the first one had, but how long would I have to wait for the second? I didn't particularly like working in architectural offices, but where else would I learn the business of building? I had been corresponding regularly with Bing, who was working for an architect in Toronto, and I thought of joining him. I remembered our earnest conversations in Ottawa. I still wanted to change the world, but I didn't know how to channel my idealism. Of course, a small island in the Mediterranean was hardly the most propitious place to change anything. On June 5, the combined forces of Egypt, Syria, and Jordan invaded Israel. I had been reading *Homage to Catalonia,* and for a brief, self-indulgent moment I considered going to Israel. I was still thinking about it when, six days later, the war was over.

The root of my problem was that I didn't know which of my Polish grandfathers' fairy tales to make my own. On the one hand, I could not shed the feeling that I should be doing something useful with my life, going to graduate school, getting a job, starting a career, getting married, settling down. At the same time, I liked the idea of retreat. For the son of immigrants—and of an ambitious mother—decisively turning one's back on the world was particularly attractive. And life in Formentera was pleasant. I had met a young French couple, Jibus and Nicolle, who were renting the house next door. They were happy to find someone to talk to—few of the Americans and English spoke French—and we struck up a friendship. It was never clear to me how they supported themselves. Jibus had once apprenticed to a painting restorer—or maybe, Jibus joked, a forger, that wasn't completely clear—but I never saw him paint, although he did give me a pair of exquisite little landscapes. "*Je voudrais que chaque jour soit une fiesta,*" he used to say. I would like every day to be a holiday. And so they were. We would go swimming together, explore the island, eat at each other's houses, and listen to music. I had bought a battery-powered tape recorder from Werner, a German hippie who had run out of money. The reel-to-reel Grundig, bulky as a portable sewing machine, came with several homemade tapes: Aretha Franklin, Percy Sledge, and other rhythm-and-blues performers. It wasn't jazz, and it certainly wasn't my father's piano, but it filled the house with music.

Jibus would sometimes make cookies or marmalade out of hashish. Marijuana and hashish were a big part of life on Formentera, as ubiquitous as cigarettes or wine. The shared hash cookie and the offered joint were part of island hospitality. I liked the convivial social atmosphere of lazy relaxation that they produced. One evening I took a tab of LSD. I knew nothing of lysergic acid diethylamide, except that it was possible to have a "bad trip," although the person who sold it assured me it was "good stuff, from California." It *was* good—at least for me. I spent most of the night sitting alone outside my house, wrapped in a blanket and surrounded by a strange and shimmering moonlit landscape, an experience that I can only describe as like being inside a van Gogh painting. The next day I walked down to La Sabina to take the launch to Ibiza. I recorded the experience: "Everything was sharp and clear and beautiful. At the dock I had an apple and a coffee. The boat came. There was a great wind. I sat in the bow and it was like no other boat trip I have ever taken. Colors, spray, and everything slowed down, so that I could see the droplets on the bow wave. The forty-five-minute trip seemed to take all day."

Eventually, matters came to a head. The weather was getting hotter, and with summer came more visitors and day trippers. It was time to leave. At the end of June, Jibus approached me with a proposal. He and Nicolle were planning to go to Marrakech, would I like to accompany them? I was tempted. I still had some money, and Morocco would probably be even cheaper than Spain. And I liked Jibus and Nicolle, who were easygoing, undemanding, and fun to be with. I could imagine myself lolling on a Marrakech rooftop with them. But finally, reluctantly, I said, Thank you, no. I had to admit that total retreat was not for me. Designing Jacques's house had been hard work, but in the process I had learned a lot about Formentera—and about myself. I wanted more of that. The hash cookies were nice, but not really a substitute. As for LSD, I was a little afraid of it—that had been *too* nice. I discovered that, unlike my friend Jibus, I didn't want every day to be a holiday. Once in a while was enough. I had tried to imitate my recluse-grandfather, but—unexpectedly—it was my banker-grandfather who asserted himself. I would go back to the world.

Melange

I spent part of the sixties working with a children's theater group. We stretched a bolt of elastic nylon fabric from floor to ceiling using rubber cords and garter belt snaps as attachments. The result, which resembled one of Frei Otto's tensile structures, was a sort of endless, magical tent.

The plot of Frank Herbert's classic science-fiction Dune trilogy revolves around a narcotic spice called melange. Melange is found only on a small, desertlike planet—Dune—which is the setting for an interplanetary trade war over control of the commodity. I was reminded of Herbert's story as I looked out on the placid blue waters of the Bay of Campeche, off the east coast of Mexico. Out at sea, the horizon was dotted with anchored ships. They were empty tankers, and they'd come from around the world to this small, out-of-the-way place to collect our civilization's version of melange—petroleum.

It was 1980. In two years, the Mexican economy would collapse, but for now it was in full swing and Mexicans were high on the euphoria of the oil boom. "It's not like Kuwait," my friend Luis Lesur, who advised the government, told me. "It's like a *big* Kuwait." The port town of Coatzacoalcos, on the Bay of Campeche, was in the heart of the Veracruz field. Helicopters belonging to PEMEX, the federal petroleum company, buzzed back and forth overhead, Japanese four-wheel-drive vehicles sped along the dusty roads, hard-hatted workers partied loudly in makeshift bars. The barren, desertlike landscape, which actually resembled Herbert's fictional planet, was dotted with shanties made from corrugated metal sheets and scrap wood. The atmosphere was at once chaotic and purposeful. The shanties were new and slapped together, both provisional and optimistic; everyone was grasping for a piece of the sudden prosperity. Nineteenth-century gold rushes must have been something like this.

I was not here for the oil. I'd come with an architect colleague on behalf of the Banco de México, which had engaged us to develop a new strategy for building housing for low-income workers. The idea was to erect precast concrete structures, in some cases only structural walls and floors, which could be filled in by the homeowners themselves, working at their own pace. This combination of industrial production and do-it-yourself improvisation was a way to harness the growing industrial capacity of Mexico and its people's traditional skills and enterprise. We were in Coatzacoalcos to scout a possible site for a trial run of what the Mexicans called *soportes de la vivienda*—housing supports. Our concept was based on work done by John Habraken, a Dutch architect then teaching at MIT.

We stayed overnight in a local "motel," a row of shacks with flimsy partitions between the rooms and a rusty water tap in the yard for washing. It was hot and miserably humid. Everything was damp. A radio blared next door, and the absence of more than a dim single lightbulb made reading impossible. We did what everyone else did in the evenings: drank beer. My colleague, Eric Dluhosch, a Czech-born Canadian, was a professor at MIT. We'd known each other for a number of years. An elegant man, who looked like a Central European diplomat, he did not consider himself a specialist in third world housing, although he had recently worked on a similar project in Egypt. "It might have turned out differently," he told me. During his first teaching job—at

Cornell—he had been asked by the School of Hotel Administration to organize an architecture class in hotel design. For a number of reasons the proposal fell through, and a few years later he moved to MIT. "I could have been a very different sort of international expert," Eric said ruefully, wiping the sweat from his brow. "I could be staying in a five-star beach hotel, instead of this dump." It was a good story, and we laughed. I could imagine how he felt, but I had no similar excuse—I was here by choice.

A dozen years earlier, when I returned to Montreal after my sojourn on Formentera, I had trouble settling down. I had decided not to lose myself in Marrakech, but I didn't really have an alternative plan. I easily found a job in an architect's office, and rented the attic floor of an old stone farmhouse beside the broad St. Lawrence River, outside the city. I was hoping to re-create my previous country life, but it didn't work. It wasn't Formentera, it was the suburbs, and I was no longer an island bohemian but a commuter. When my lease ran out, I moved downtown. Over the next four years I lived in four different flats, now in one neighborhood, now in another. I was still traveling.

It never occurred to me to leave Montreal. Although I kept in touch with Ralph and Andrejs, I didn't have a lot of old friends there—Hugh and Tony had graduated and left the city, and though I sometimes saw Bing, he was in Toronto. Montreal in 1968 was a cosmopolitan place. The world's fair had been a great success, and the city was preparing to host the 1976 Olympics. There were plenty of jobs for a young architect; it was only a question of what one wanted to do. I changed employers as often as apartments. First I worked in a large office that was planning a town for hydroelectric workers in northern Labrador. Two of us worked as lead designers on the project: Frank Hamilton was responsible for the town center, I for the houses. Our *patron,* Edouard Fiset, was a courtly French Canadian whose father had been lieutenant-governor of the province. Fiset rarely came into the drafting room where we worked, and, when he did, he walked between the drawing tables hardly saying a word. We were intimidated by him, but I think he was merely shy. After a year, work slowed down in the office and people started getting laid off. Frank—an unruly employee—was sure that he was next. He wrote an elaborate letter of resignation, and carried it in his breast pocket for a week. Finally he was called to Fiset's office—and offered a raise. I was kept on, too, but as there didn't seem to be interesting work in the offing, I decided it was time to leave.

The bistro on Mountain Street where Ed Satterthwaite and I had spent our evenings was still an architects' hangout. Andy Morrison, a furniture designer from Virginia, whom I then knew only slightly, told me that he was building models for an architect who was transforming what had been the United States pavilion at Expo into an aviary. He was looking for an architectural assistant. I thought that Buckminster Fuller's geodesic dome was one of the most interesting buildings at the fair—along with Habitat and Frei Otto's giant tent structure, which housed the German pavilion—so I applied and was hired. The new job was a change. There were only three of us. Our employer, Luis Villa, was a Colombian architect who had studied at Penn and come to Montreal to work on the fair. We designed mammoth birdcages using chain-link fencing suspended from the lacy dome. Visiting the construction site, and seeing something I'd drawn on paper actually built, was exciting.

After the aviary was completed, I stayed on to work with Luis on two smaller projects: landscaping for the American embassy in Bogotá, and a house for his sister in Medellín. Eventually, the work ran out and Luis left on an extended trip to Colombia. He spoke vaguely about what we might do when he returned, but essentially I was out of a job. At loose ends, I ran into Norbert Schoenauer, whose office was planning a large housing development in Quebec City. Would I be interested in being project architect? he asked. Norbert, a Hungarian, had been one of my favorite teachers, and I was flattered. "Project architect" was a grand title, since there were only two of us on the job, but I had a lot of freedom and it was like being back in school: sketching, building models, discussing architecture. We completed the preliminary design and started to work on a new mining town in Labrador. I met the celebrated Swedish architect Ralph Erskine, who was brought in as an adviser. Considering that I had never been north of the Mont Tremblant ski resort, I was learning a lot about sub-Arctic living.

After a year, the design work on the northern town was complete, and I decided to move on. There was a job opening in Safdie's office, where I had worked after graduation, and I returned to modular housing. The office had grown, and there were more projects—versions of Habitat for New York City, Puerto Rico, Israel, and the Virgin Islands. Safdie continued to be fascinated by three-dimensional geometry. It had been hard enough to build the original Habitat, which was composed of stacked-up concrete boxes; now the prefabricated units were tetrahedrons and octahedrons. Safdie would make sketches, which the office would turn into complicated models and drawings. It was engaging work but elusive, for nothing ever seemed to get built. Sometimes it was unclear even if the projects *could* be built.

I liked working for Safdie, who was by far the most inventive architect I had ever met, and who attracted interesting employees, but I wasn't sure I was really learning anything useful. I had thought of returning to graduate school, and had applied and been accepted by the University of Oregon, but I changed my mind at the last minute. A friend of mine had gone to study with Paolo Soleri, a visionary architect who had an architectural compound in Arizona, and he spoke highly of the experience. A planning school in Athens sounded interesting. Since I had saved some money, I decided to take a break and consider my options.

Shortly after I left Safdie's office, he called me to say that he had a client who wanted him to do the interior design of his office. It was too small a job for him, Safdie said, but would I be interested? By then I had my architectural license. Of course, I said yes—what young architect wouldn't? My client was Bill Sofin, a glamorous Montreal businessman who owned a chain of pharmacies and had created a famous Montreal nightclub in the sixties called Le Drug. My design for his office was ambitious for a novice and included curved walls, concealed sliding doors, and exposed air-conditioning ducts on the ceilings. When the owner of the building protested, Sofin put his arm around me and said: "This is what my architect wants, and this is what we will do." Sofin was infuriatingly tardy in paying his bills—I was always one project behind in collecting my fees—but that one remark made up for a lot. Over the next year, I designed not only his office but also two of his stores.

Architecture has sometimes been called a social art, referring to the fact that buildings fulfill a social function. But the profession of architect is social in another way: to build, an architect needs clients. Especially at the beginning of one's career, clients are generally drawn from one's immediate social circle—parents, relatives, friends of the family, classmates, neighbors. It is rare that an architect finances his own first project, although the celebrated Philadelphia architect George Howe jump-started his career by building houses for himself, as did Philip Johnson. Many architects begin by building a house for their parents: Robert Venturi, Charles Gwathmey, and Richard Meier, all built their first projects for Mom and Dad.

I had already done that. Shortly after returning from Europe, I built a summer cottage for my parents in Vermont, on North Hero Island, overlooking Lake Champlain. I based the plan on a long, narrow house that Le Corbusier had built for *his* parents beside Lake Geneva in 1925, except that, since my design was built out of cedar logs, it was more Natty Bumppo than Bauhaus Modern. The tongue-and-groove, notched logs were manufactured by the Pan-Abode company in British Columbia, which precut the pieces—walls, floor, and roof—to my design and shipped them to Vermont in a boxcar. Ralph Bergman, my old classmate and traveling companion, helped me with the construction. Each log was numbered, and once we had sorted them out, it took only two weeks to put it all together. It was like a huge game of Lincoln Logs.

But my parents' house did not lead to other work. Their immigrant friends were not in a position to commission buildings. Bill Sofin had dropped into my lap by accident—as had happened once before in Formentera—but having grown up in St. Johns, I had no social connections in Montreal. Most of the people I knew were other architects, and while my Loyola classmates might have provided useful contacts, I had long since lost touch with them.

Lacking potential clients, I invented my own. I had become friends with two actors, Fred Smith and Sidonie Kerr, who ran a children's theater group. Their ideas about theater were influenced by the European Adventure Playground movement, by Bertolt Brecht, and by the writings of the French visionary actor and playwright Antonin Artaud, who advocated breaking down the barriers between audience and actors. Fred and Sidonie's theater was not *for* children but *with* children. There was no audience, and no script—the "play" was improvised. The children would be given an imaginary starting point—"we're on a canoe trip" or "we're going down into a mine"—and the story would then be allowed to take its course. Our role was to be a part of the action, to react to the children's suggestions, and to nudge the "plot" along at decisive moments.

I started taking part in the play and found I enjoyed it. It was a bit like performing jazz, for the children were natural and endless improvisers, daring us to keep up. "I just saw something, there in the corner. What is it? I think it's a dragon. Is it friendly? No, it's charging at us, run! Let's go though this secret panel."

One memorable outdoor session involved more than a hundred children at a summer day camp outside the city. The story was that the world was coming to an end and we had to collect "stuff" to take with us on a rocket ship to outer space—Noah's Ark. There were six or eight adults, and we split into several groups to track down and collect whatever the children thought was valuable cargo to take on the voyage. At first the kids were judicious in their choices—a dog, a pony, a box of toys—but soon caution was thrown to the wind, and the animals and objects grew outrageously large, requiring teamwork and considerable heaving and hauling. Everything was brought to a large clearing. At the end of the hour, we all met together to prepare for takeoff. Fred had borrowed a NASA tape recording of a real launch, countdown and all. "Five, four, three, two, one!" the children yelled in unison. The roar of the rocket engines boomed over the loudspeakers, and we all blasted off into space.

Most play sessions were considerably smaller and took place in a downtown loft. There were no props in our play, everything was imagined. Once in a while we would use something like an old cardboard packing case, or a blanket draped over a table, to create a physical setting. I thought that these makeshift devices could be improved upon. Fred had gotten his hands on a bolt of elastic nylon fabric, and using rubber cords and garter belt snaps as attachments, we stretched the fabric between walls and floors. The result, which resembled one of Frei Otto's tensile structures, was a sort of endless, magical tent (the fabric was red). The whole thing could be easily and quickly set up or taken down, had no predetermined shape, and, being soft and flexible, allowed children to run into it without hurting themselves. I designed a second structure of slotted half-inch-thick corrugated cardboard panels that could be used to build large houses of cards. I called them Dynamods—dynamic modules (I was reading Buckminster Fuller at the time). I had a vague idea of marketing the toy but never got beyond drawing up a promotional brochure.

I spent a happy year in this make-believe world. I enjoyed playing with the children, messing about with the Dynamods, and hanging out with Fred and Sidonie. Both had worked at the National Film Board (Sidonie later became a director and writer), and Fred occasionally borrowed films and set up a projector in the loft (this was before videotapes) to screen old documentaries. I had liked the theater—

and theater people—ever since working backstage in productions in high school and college. I was in no hurry to go back to work in an office. My savings, and the income from my small architectural commissions, paid the rent on my downtown flat and kept an old Mini Cooper in running order. My free time was spent reading Fuller and listening to recordings of Brecht plays, in hindsight an odd combination. I fell in and out of love with depressing regularity. (Claudia had met someone else and moved to Boston.) I suppose I was waiting for something to happen.

Something did. That year I was teaching part-time at the McGill School of Architecture, and I occasionally attended evening lectures by visiting architects. Which is how I met Alvaro Ortega. Ortega, a Colombian, was a housing expert with the United Nations, and the subject of his talk was low-cost building around the world. He dressed like a UN bureaucrat, in a dark suit and tie, but when he spoke it became clear that his ideas were anything but conventional. He showed slides of delicate reinforced concrete roofs that he had built in Colombia and explained how he had made them thinner and thinner, until they had collapsed. The audience laughed, but he wasn't joking. "You can learn more from a building that falls down than from one that stands up," he said.

I had never encountered anyone quite like him.

Most architects are keen to prove the inevitability of whatever they design, and when they call something "experimental," they generally mean "unusual." Ortega was different. He really was experimenting. The next day, I made an appointment to see him. It turned out that he had an office at McGill. He told me that he was here on a three-year leave of absence and had received a grant from the Canadian federal government to start a graduate research program. The research concerned something he called "minimum cost housing," by which he meant housing for the world's poor. Except for a brief holiday in Mexico, I had never been in a third world country, but I liked Ortega, and his no-nonsense approach. He was obviously someone who was interested in doing things, not just talking about them. He had funds for two graduate scholarships and invited me to apply. It was 1970, what some referred to as "alternative architecture"—a legacy of the turbulent sixties—was in the wind, and Ortega's ambitious program appealed to my youthful idealism. In short order I became his first student, enrolled in a two-year master of architecture program. I had no idea that minimum cost housing would consume the next two decades of my life.

Another thing that attracted me to Ortega was his cosmopolitan background, as checkered as my own. Born in Bogotá, he had been an architecture student in Paris when the Second World War broke out and had come to McGill to finish his degree. After doing graduate work at Harvard—during the glory days of Walter Gropius and Marcel Breuer—he returned to Bogotá to practice architecture. Like many Colombians, he was driven out of the country by La Violencia, the civil war of the late forties and fifties, and joined the Housing, Building and Planning Branch of the United Nations. His work was to advise local governments on technical aspects of housing. His greatest success during this period was developing the *canaletta,* a thin asbestos-cement corrugated roof. Ortega had worked in Latin America, Africa, the Middle East, and South Asia. He truly was, in that hackneyed phrase, a citizen of the world.

Ortega was my teacher, but he was not an academic. We didn't have classes or seminars; in any case there were only three of us—the other student was Samir Ayad, an Egyptian. We started right in doing practical work. One of Ortega's pet ideas was to use an atomizer for washing as a way of reducing domestic consumption of water. This device was originally invented by Buckminster Fuller, who called it a "fog gun." The principle was to atomize water into fine droplets—a mist, really—which were particularly effective in cleaning the skin but used only a tiny amount of water. Ortega wanted to simplify Fuller's device so that it could be used by people who didn't have running water—or electricity. We experimented with an assortment of hand-pumped atomizers, paint and garden sprayers, and aerosol nozzles, measuring water consumption and washing effectiveness. NASA had developed an atomized zero-gravity shower for space flight, but we were looking for something much simpler. Eventually we built an inexpensive portable mist shower using off-the-shelf plastic plumbing fixtures, pressurized with a bicycle pump.

Another of Ortega's longtime obsessions was finding a way to use sulfur as a building material. Sulfur is available as a volcanic ore and as a by-product of petroleum refining. When melted and combined with sand and gravel, sulfur becomes a kind of cement, and it cools as a hard concretelike material. Sulfur concrete has a number of unusual properties: it is nonporous and waterproof, it can be easily recycled, and it takes a smooth finish—we called it "poor man's marble." We jury-rigged a cement mixer with a propane burner and mixed sulfur with various aggregates, performing tests on samples in McGill's engineering lab but also making washbasins and building blocks. We experimented with molds of wood, steel, and glass. We built a section of paving on the campus using interlocking sulfur blocks to see how different aggregates resisted foot traffic. There was no right way or wrong way to use sulfur. We tried spraying it as a coating, using it as a glue, and impregnating cardboard and paper in sulfur baths. It wasn't so different from my play with Fred and Sidonie: improvisation, trying whatever came to mind, making do with whatever was at hand—what the French call *bricolage*—messing about. We got most of our "equipment" from a downtown kitchen supply store.

We soon discovered a number of drawbacks to building with sulfur, chiefly that not only was it flammable but when burning it produced noxious sulfur dioxide. Ortega, undeterred, maintained that the acrid smell was a built-in fire alarm. We experimented with various fire retardants that made the material self-extinguishing. We weren't discouraged. Invention demands a suspension of disbelief—you can't solve all the problems at once. Ortega used to say that there were two types of people: Mr. Yes and Mr. No. Mr. Yes was willing to try new things; Mr. No was stuck in place. We weren't sure exactly how sulfur would be used, but we were confident that eventually some practical applications would be found. Meanwhile, we forged ahead. Our white lab coats had "Friends of Sulfur" stenciled on the back.

Our first full-scale construction project was a small house, built on the university's suburban agricultural campus. The structure incorporated a number of devices and techniques we had been working on: mortarless interlocking blocks and flooring tiles of sulfur, rooftop solar stills to purify bathwater, rainwater collection devices, and an electricity-generating wind machine. We did all the construction ourselves—by now there were other graduate students: Arthur Acheson from Northern Ireland, Salama Saad from Egypt, Mamadou Bob from Senegal, and Wajid Ali—who was later best man at my wedding—from Pakistan. We dug the footings, cast the blocks, and built a toilet that flushed with dirty water from the sink. When we were finished, Arthur and his wife, Elizabeth, spent seven weeks living in the house and monitoring the various systems. One of the project's many visitors was Buckminster Fuller. "What are you going to call the house?" he asked. We admitted that we didn't have a name for what we generally referred to as the "ecological house." Fuller sat down, thought for a few minutes, and christened it the Ecol Operation.

This was 1972—a year before the energy crisis. By then I had completed my master's degree, but I was hooked. I stayed on as a research associate, and when Ortega returned to the United Nations, I took his place. More students came, from India, Iran, Egypt, Saudi Arabia, Venezuela, Brazil, England, Hungary, Switzerland, Canada, and the United States. We did our work in a series of garages and coach houses that belonged to the university. They were usually slated for demolition, at which point we packed our tools and moved on to the next premises. We did research on sulfur concrete and retractable greenhouse insulation. One student wrote his thesis on solar water heaters made out of black trash bags; another built and tested an atomized shower. We developed roofing shingles made out of corrugated cardboard impregnated with sulfur. We looked for ways to recycle waste materials into buildings by designing reusable bottles and cans. We experimented with composting toilets and designed a do-it-yourself version. Some of the experiments worked, and some didn't—as Ortega had pointed out, we learned from our failures. We took the work, but not ourselves, very seriously.

The activities of what was now called the Minimum Cost Housing Group were not confined to the laboratory. We built a shelter on a Cree reservation in Alberta and a small house for a children's summer camp outside Montreal. I took a leave of absence and spent a year working on a World Bank project on low-cost sanitation. I helped Ortega with a UN project in a Manila slum. I traveled as a consultant to northern Ontario (another Cree community), Nigeria, Tanzania, and India.

I liked the work, not only because it felt useful (and was actually a lot of fun) but also because concentrating on the problems of people in far-off places paradoxically made me feel less of an outsider. Or at least the work turned my outsider status to advantage. Sometimes, looking at situations afresh, I could see new possibilities. For example, we surveyed several slums in the Indian city of Indore and discovered that, while the population density was extremely high—as we expected—the houses were not all small; many were quite large, since the extended families often included a dozen or more people. This suggested that providing tiny house plots, as the World Bank and most aid agencies were doing, was not the most effective solution. We developed a planning strategy that took heterogeneity into account and could grow in an organic manner. We called it the No-Plan Plan. The aim was to find a way for planned settlements to grow more naturally, as unplanned communities did, that is, to build improvisation into the process. Which is all part of what had brought me to the Bay of Campeche and Coatzacoalcos.

The Boathouse

Hemmingford, fall 1977. Despite the glowing prose of do-it-yourself manuals, building your own house is characterized not only by fulfillment but also by bouts of depression. Lacking experience, I made mistakes and had to redo work, sometimes several times, which could be demoralizing. Eventually, Shirley and I started to take "vacations" from our project, which sometimes felt like a Sisyphean penance.

Sooner or later, an architect should build a house for himself. I did, although in a rather roundabout fashion. I have always been fascinated by boats. When I was a teenager, living in St. Johns, I sent away to *Popular Mechanics* for a set of do-it-yourself plans for a plywood sailing dinghy. The magazine assured me that it could be built by "anyone with a hammer and saw," which was about the extent of my father's tool kit. The construction went smoothly, my mother sewed a nylon sail, and in short order I launched the boat on the Richelieu. Rather than make a test run, however, I decided to sail ten miles downriver. The embarrassing result was a tremendous case of sunburn, following a windless afternoon spent drifting on a half-submerged, leaky hull that was so heavy even the current had difficulty moving it. The boat spent the rest of its life on dry land, in the back of my parents' garage.

Now, fifteen years later, I wanted to have another go. I subscribed to *WoodenBoat,* read books on boatbuilding, and wrote away for study plans. I was an accomplished model maker, and soon my study contained a small armada of cardboard sailing boats, with masts made out of chopsticks and billowing paper sails. When I had more or less settled on a design—a twenty-five-foot ketch—I realized that I needed a place to build. Finding a workshop where I lived, in downtown Montreal, would be expensive, since I needed the space for an extended period of time—judging from what I had read, several years. One book suggested building an impermanent wood-and-plastic shelter, a sort of greenhouse, which would last the necessary time and could then be easily taken down.

But where? City land was too expensive, I would have to find something in the country. That summer, my wife, Shirley, and I spent several weekends driving about one hour—forty-five miles—from Montreal in different directions. To the northwest, the Laurentian Mountains were attractive, and there were many small lakes, but the area had long since been taken over by ski resorts and vacation homes. North of the city was emptier but too wild; I wanted to build a boat, not become a pioneer. To the west, the landscape was flat and characterless. That left the south.

Hemmingford is a village a few miles from the American border. The local real estate agent showed us what he optimistically called "mini-farms": parcels of uncultivated land that real farmers had long since abandoned. Dismayed at our indifference, he suggested that there was one other piece of land we ought to see—an apple grower was selling off the corner of his orchard. It was October, and there were apples on the ground as we walked among the trees. What we saw when we emerged from the orchard was a long, flat meadow and beyond it a field, bounded on the far side by a hedgerow. When we reached the end of the meadow, where the flat land broke and started a gentle slope to a far-off hill, we stopped under a solitary old apple tree to admire the bucolic view. The agent pointed out the boundaries of the parcel. Shirley and I looked at each other and knew that we had found the place.

By the time the legal paperwork for the land sale was concluded, it was late fall. Soon it would be winter, the ground would be frozen, and construction would be impossible. In any case, buying the land had severely depleted our savings, so it was hardly the time to think of building. During that winter, my sketchbook filled up with drawings of sheds of various types.

The following summer we regularly spent weekends on our property, pitching a tent in the meadow. I didn't start building; instead I bought a slab of wood from the local sawmill and made a picnic table, which we set up under the apple tree. It was a modest enough start, but I was in no hurry. At the end of the summer, we invited our friend Vikram Bhatt, an Indian architect who worked with me in the Minimum Cost Housing Group, to spend the day with us in the country. After lunch, the three of us sat at the picnic table, talking. I told him about my plans for the boatbuilding workshop. I was probably showing off a little and making it sound more definite than it really was. So I was taken aback when he said, "Why don't you at least put in a foundation this year? If you did it yourself, it wouldn't cost very much. I have some free time just now—we could do it together."

Why not? I was leaving in three weeks, to do a monthlong project with Ortega in the Philippines, but I didn't want to pass up Vikram's generous offer. We would have to start immediately. Although I didn't have a final plan for the workshop, I knew the size of the boat, so I could estimate the dimensions of the building. We could build a concrete slab now, and I would have the rest of the winter to figure out exactly what would go on top of it. We sited the building, a sixteen-by-thirty-two-foot rectangle, not far from the old apple tree. I hired a neighbor with a bulldozer to scrape off the grass and a layer of topsoil, which we replaced by crushed stone. We built a wood form, laid down a polyethylene sheet as a moisture barrier, a mesh of reinforcing steel, and edge insulation, and put in heavier bars to reinforce the edges. There was some wood left over, and we added a small rectangle at one end—to accommodate a sauna, which I thought would be useful after a long day of boatbuilding.

This work was interrupted by a week of heavy rain, which made the field soggy, so the truck delivering sand and gravel got stuck halfway and had to dump its load several hundred feet from the building site. I borrowed a tractor from a neighboring apple grower, and we laboriously transported the materials to where we had installed a cement mixer. Then we loaded sand, gravel, and cement into the mixer, fetching drums of water from the neighbor's house. Vikram and I shoveled the concrete mix into the form, and Shirley troweled it smooth. We rushed through the work in two days—all the time I had before my departure for Manila—leaving the three of us exhausted, too exhausted for any sense of achievement.

I intended to resume construction the following year, and I spent the winter exploring alternative designs. Vikram and I had reduced the dimensions of the concrete slab to a minimum, leaving only enough space for building the boat hull. I would have a loft—for storing materials—at one end of the workshop and a sleeping loft above the future sauna at the other end.

A sleeping loft sounds simple enough, but I soon decided I would need at least a few basic amenities: a toilet, a shower, and space for a pump and a water heater. Although I planned the compact living quarters like a ship's cabin, I found I needed extra space, so I reduced the length of the workshop by two feet. What about a place for hanging clothes? And room for a ship's ladder to the loft? The workshop shrank by another two feet. Anxiously, I checked my boat plans. I would have to squeeze myself around the bow and stern, but it would do—just barely.

The scale of the workshop—its high ceiling, wide

doors, and the greater span of its structure—was quite different from the snug cubbyholes of the living quarters. I started to emphasize this difference in my designs. I was thinking of a clerestory or skylights instead of windows, and since the workshop did not have to be well insulated, the walls could be inexpensive cement blocks. In my work with the Minimum Cost Housing Group, we had used sulfur instead of mortar, and I thought I might try that. The living quarters remained framed in wood. In my sketches, the two little buildings stood side by side, in uneasy intimacy.

There is sometimes a moment in the design process when exploring many options has not produced a satisfactory solution and the architect must reconsider his initial assumptions. It was obvious that something had to be done about the competition for space that had developed between the living quarters and the workshop. For some time I had been concerned that my plan to build a twenty-five-foot ketch was too ambitious. There was another design that appealed to me, a twenty-foot catboat, which would allow me to further reduce the length of the workshop. Now the living quarters occupied more than a third of the concrete slab.

Having resolved the question of size, I turned my attention to the appearance of the building. My latest sketches showed an unsentimental, flat-roofed structure, taller at one end, and resembling a boot.

The result looked . . . well, "functional" was a kind description. Since the slab was in the middle of a flat meadow, there were no trees—except for the solitary apple—to mask the building, no hillock to shelter against, no place to hide. The workshop would be fully visible from the road, about eight hundred feet away, as one approached across the meadow. And what did my hard little industrial building have to do with the surrounding farms? Very little. Ten years earlier, Mike Shaw had told me, "Your house doesn't look much like the other houses on the island." I realized with dismay that much the same could be said of my present project. I had to face it: this ungainly little building would stick out like the proverbial sore thumb.

It had been easy for me, as a foreigner, to observe the architectural language of the Formentera houses, but here—at home—I had been taking my surroundings for granted. There were two types of buildings in the Hemmingford vicinity: farmhouses and barns. A barn and a workshop are not so different, I reasoned. The local barns were long, simple structures with few openings in their wooden walls, and while they were usually parts of farmyards, they sometimes stood alone, in the middle of a field—just like my workshop. Looking through a book on the history of barns in North America, I came across a photograph of a barn overlooking the St. Lawrence River, on the Île d'Orléans, near Quebec City. What caught my eye was the uncompromising way the prosaic building presented its broad face to the viewer: no cupolas, no decorations, no sheltering overhangs, in fact, no "architectural" features of any kind. Its form recalled its Breton ancestry: the so-called connected barn, in which different functions—hay storage, threshing floor, cattle shed, stables, and sometimes even the house itself—were placed under one long roof. The Île d'Orléans barn had a number of different doors: full-height for hay wagons, large double doors leading into the hayloft, other doors to allow animals into the byre, and a small opening obviously intended for humans. The pragmatic adaptation of size to function reminded me of the Formentera houses.

I kept returning to this photograph, until I realized that what I was looking at could be my boat-building workshop. Of course, I planned to use the floor for lofting, not threshing, and to accommodate a boat, not a hay cart, but the way the connected barn pragmatically housed different functions under a single roof appealed to me. The large roof gave dignity to this otherwise modest building. I also liked the spare fenestration and air of frugal restraint. After almost two years, and two sketchbooks full of designs, I was going to build . . . a barn.

Once I decided on a barnlike shape, it was easy to fit the two main functions within it—boatbuilding at one end, living at the other. I needed large doors to get the boat out of the workshop, and I put them in the gable wall; a small door provided access at the other end. I placed a window over the big doors to let light into the workshop, but the living area needed more windows. Windows were a problem, since the beauty of a barn is precisely that it has large blank walls; put too many windows in, and it starts to look like a house. I made only one large window—as large as a barn door—facing south, which could be shared by both floors of the living quarters.

Taking the barn as a model produced not only an uncomplicated building form but also a simple and economic structure. The two long walls would carry a series of trussed rafters, resembling large A's, spanning the width of the building and supporting the gable roof. This solution had a number of advantages. A steep roof not only sheds water and snow effectively but also allows rooms on the upper floor—lofts, in my case—to be situated within the roof, like an attic, which reduces the height of the external walls and the interior volume of the building. Cheaper to build, and cheaper to heat, too.

We started that summer. Vikram and I built the walls out of two-by-fours, nailing them together on the ground and tilting them up into place. The roof trusses were likewise assembled on the concrete slab, which served as a large worktable. I loved this part of the work. Compared with concrete, a nasty, inert material, wood is—or at least has been—alive. It has a smell and a feel that are pleasurable. So was the rhythm of the framing process, which alternated between the energetic driving of nails, and the slower and more exacting operation of measuring and cutting. When we stopped, as we did often, the tapping of hammers and the scraping of saws were replaced by the meadow sounds of birdsong and chirping crickets. Our surroundings heightened the feeling of being pioneers. So did the fact that we were working with hand tools. There was no electricity on the site, and I had resisted renting a noisy generator. Building by hand was a romantic idea—and one I wouldn't repeat—but we were pioneers. When we were finished, this particular place would be changed forever: the meadow would be occupied.

It took us only a few weeks to complete the framing and to nail on the sheathing that braced the spindly studs and rafters and turned the skeletal structure into something that resembled a building. We laid the asphalt shingles, a tedious and unpleasant job, which required balancing precariously on what I now wished was a less steep roof. After Vikram left to visit his brother in California, Shirley and I installed the windows. I put up the vertical cedar siding that covered the exterior. By the end of the summer, we had completed what builders call the shell. I nailed plywood over the door openings and left the building for the winter.

It took us the following summer to finish the interior. I replaced the awkward ladder to the sleeping loft by a steep, narrow staircase. This lopped a couple more feet off the workshop but left space for a sitting alcove and a storage cupboard under the stairs. I insulated the living quarters and installed a chimney and a wood-burning stove. The back door came from a salvage yard. The workshop was unheated and uninsulated, but it had one distinctive feature: flanking the large doors in the gable end we built two walls made out of bottles set in cement. Shirley and I had been collecting bottles for the last three years: wine bottles, gallon jugs, gin and scotch bottles, and four jeroboams safeguarded since our wedding. On the exterior, the ends of the bottles made a pleasant pattern of different-size circles; inside, especially as the sun set, the bottle walls blazed with amber and emerald colors. On the oval brown bottom of an Armagnac bottle, I engraved MCMLXXVII RYBCZYNSKI FECIT as well as the names of my co-workers.

The building was finished; I was pleased with its appearance. As I had hoped, the general effect was distinctly agricultural and suited the surroundings. The north wall offered a blank face to the public road; a chance passerby would scarcely give it a glance. On the other side, the single large window overlooking the meadow provided a generous scale. The cedar boards were turning gray, and the unobtrusive little barn already looked at home.

* * *

Now there were no more excuses, no more putting things off, it was time to start building my boat. I took the roll of naval blueprints down from the top of the bookshelf in my study, where I had left it three years ago. The drawings still showed a stubby catboat, with a broad beam and a roomy cockpit. I studied the table of offsets and the list of materials, and familiarized myself once more with the arcane vocabulary of boatbuilding. My first step would be lofting, that is, transferring the dimensions from the drawings to sheets of paper, to provide full-size templates for the frames that made up the skeleton of the hull. The frames were made of two-by-fours, just like my workshop, but mahogany, not pine; the hull was plywood, although marine grade and fastened with bronze screws, not common nails.

I should have been in a hurry to begin, but as I commenced these preparations, I realized that, although the drawings hadn't changed, I had. As I read the naval architect's instructions, I imagined myself sawing wood and pounding nails—or, at least, screwing screws. I was surprised to find that I wasn't looking forward to it. What had previously promised to be a pleasurable pastime was starting to feel like a chore. Perhaps—subconsciously—I also remembered that hapless teenager floating down the Richelieu.

Looking back on it, I can now see more clearly

what had originally pushed me into this workshop-building project. It wasn't really about boats; I just wanted to build something for myself, with my own hands. This impulse originated from economic necessity, but I enjoyed doing each step of the process, experiencing at first hand the transformation from sketch to reality. I also found that certain architectural decisions—the precise location of a window, the height of a ceiling, the detail at an eave—were best made on the building site, by the builder himself.

But now that I had done it, I had to admit to a sense of weariness as well as satisfaction. Despite the glowing prose of do-it-yourself manuals, building on your own is characterized not only by fulfillment but also by bouts of depression. The work drags on, and for every agreeable task, like framing, there is one that is merely drudgery, like installing insulation. Lacking experience, I had made mistakes and had had to redo work, sometimes several times, which could be demoralizing. Shirley and I grew cranky; she called it "Hemmingforditis." Eventually we started to take "vacations" from our project, which sometimes felt like a Sisyphean penance.

Our marriage survived, but I had no desire to test it further. It seemed to me that the boatbuilding would have to be postponed, or even abandoned. When I shamefacedly broached the subject with Shirley, my suggestion was greeted with neither dismay nor exasperation but cheerful approbation. She had always accepted my boatbuilding scheme with tolerance rather than enthusiasm, and although she didn't say "Finally, you've come to your senses"—at least not immediately—I could see she was relieved. So was I.

If I wasn't going to build a boat, I obviously didn't need a workshop, so what would be the fate of my little barn? Shirley and I had discussed one day building a country house in Hemmingford. This possibility had become more real as we spent time in the pleasant rural setting, and as we became involved not only in the construction of the workshop but also in taking care of our orchard and establishing a garden. We didn't want this to be a weekend retreat, however; we wanted to make it our permanent home. The problem was that three years had tempered our enthusiasm for building, and we were not sure if we were really up to another bout of construction. Then I had a thought: Maybe there didn't need to be any more building. What if, instead of adding a house to the workshop, we turned the workshop into a house?

The volume of space that we had built was the equivalent of a small house. I examined the possibility of turning the large workroom into a kitchen and eating area. I would have to add some partition walls and cut out some additional windows, but it could be done. The sleeping loft could gain a closet and become the bedroom. The small room below could be turned into a sitting room, although we would have to lose the sitting alcove, which would house the bulky water heater. We did not need a two-story kitchen, so I could insert a floor into the tall room, creating space on the upper level for a bathroom (lit by a new skylight). The space under the bathroom could accommodate a composting toilet. The addition of a closet and a piece of wall turned the loft that had been intended for storing boatbuilding materials into a spare bedroom, reached by an open balcony from which you could look down into the kitchen below. If I added a tall window to the kitchen, you could even see down the driveway.

The happy winter I had spent sketching options for the original boatbuilding workshop had been a solitary time, for I had been designing for myself. Shirley was willing to assist in the construction, but she did not take a great interest in the design. Now this changed. She still helped—taping and plastering the wallboard joints became her responsibility—but there were also questions, objections, demands. Once we decided that we would live here, she was not going to put up with improvisation and make-do solutions. I found myself having to explain what I was doing—and what I was going to do. Although I put up a brave professional front, she was more knowledgeable about domestic design than I—not about construction but about the details, the minutiae of everyday life that go together to make a home.

There was the question of kitchen flooring, for example. Shirley wanted a material that would require little maintenance. Left to her own devices, she would have opted for something that resembled a car wash, and could be hosed down once a week. My concern was different. Since the sitting room, dining area, and kitchen flowed into one another, and since I already had a variety of ceiling heights, I wanted a uniform flooring material to tie things together. We had painted the concrete slab, but our amateur troweling was too crude to leave exposed. We finally decided on rough clay tiles, which could be, if not hosed down, at least mopped, and which would serve equally well in the sitting room and in the kitchen.

I left plumbing and electricity until the end. The former proved simpler than I expected, thanks to plastic fittings and flexible tubing, which eliminated the mysteries of soldering and sweating copper pipe. Electricity was more problematic. Despite my father's best efforts, it remained a mystery to me, so I had to rely on a local electrician to install the entry box and the wiring. This was prudent, but I felt sorry to have to engage a professional; it was like having a trespasser in the house.

It was two more years before we finished, for by now we had learned to pace ourselves, and when the work threatened to overwhelm us, we would abandon it for a week or two. Eventually, the walls were plastered and painted, the sloped ceiling covered in cedar, and an Italian neighbor laid a tile floor over the concrete slab. There was little to remind us of the boatbuilding workshop, except for the large double doors at the end of the kitchen.

After we moved in, there were the inevitable small adjustments, as design came face-to-face with reality: a handrail added to the narrow stair, the need for an insulated curtain to reduce winter heat loss through the large window. The biggest adjustment was something I had not anticipated. It was Shirley who pointed it out. "You know that our home doesn't really look like a house," she said. The long, simple volume with its gray wood walls was unmistakably a barn, without any of the familiar signs of habitation, such as porches, shutters, or distinctive chimneys (there was a prefabricated metal chimney, but it was hardly domestic-looking). The gable roof was unbroken by dormers; indeed, the severe north wall, which was now the "front" of our house, contained only two windows, one of which was a tall, narrow slot—not very homey.

The utilitarian appearance was softened the following year, when we added a screened porch off the kitchen at the west end. The slowly maturing garden helped, too. Eventually I realized that what was conspicuously absent in our house was a front door.

When the building had still been a workshop, I had located a door at the east end. What I had always thought of as the "back door" was now the front, but it was invisible to anyone approaching the house. The importance of a front door is not only functional—the visitor needs to know where to come in—but also symbolic—it marks the threshold between public and private. The front door is the place for the social ceremonies of arrival and departure, for familial hugs and adolescent good-night kisses. It is the memory of these that gives front doors personality—that is why we adorn them with Christmas wreaths and Thanksgiving corn.

The opportunity to do something about the front door came two years after we moved. Since our house didn't have a basement, we needed a place to put a freezer, and to store firewood, apple-picking ladders, and gardening tools. In addition, as I was spending more time writing, I needed a proper study. I extended the little barn sixteen feet to the east. On the ground floor, the unheated storage space was separated from the house by a breezeway. The study was on the second floor, off the bedroom.

In the process of building the addition, I relocated the front door so that it now opened into the breezeway. But a breezeway alone was not enough to signify "house." I built a small portico that protruded from the long north wall. The supporting posts added human scale to the blank façade. The portico was what architects call a transition space, not quite inside, not altogether outside—a place to greet visitors and exchange final good-byes. I made the portico roof out of corrugated fiberglass. In the evening the translucent plastic glowed like a giant lantern, a welcoming sight as I returned home. Not a Palladian villa in Galicia, but it would do.

BIBLIOGRAPHICAL NOTES AND ACKNOWLEDGMENTS

On Polish history in general, I consulted Norman Davies's *God's Playground: A History of Poland in Two Volumes* (New York: Columbia University Press, 1982) and Adam Zamoyski's *The Polish Way: A Thousand-Year History of the Poles and Their Culture* (London: John Murray, 1987). The description of Poles in wartime Scotland is from Ksawery Pruszyński's *Poland Fights Back*, trans. Peter Jordan (London: Hodder & Stoughton, 1941). Churchill's reference to the "ministry of ungentlemanly warfare" is from M. R. D. Foot, *SOE: An Outline History of the Special Operations Executive, 1940–46* (London: British Broadcasting Corporation, 1984). For other background on the Special Operations Executive, I relied on Józef Garliński's *Poland, SOE and the Allies*, trans. Paul Stevenson (London: George Allen and Unwin, 1969) and W. J. M. Mackenzie, *The Secret History of SOE: The Special Operations Executive, 1940–1945* (London: St. Ermin's Press, 2000). Stanisław Sosabowski's *Freely I Served* (Nashville: Battery Press, 1982) casts light on the First Independent Parachute Brigade, as does Marek Swięcicki's *With the Red Devils at Arnhem* (London: MaxLove Publishing, 1945). For background on the Warsaw Uprising, I read Jan M. Ciechanowski's *The Warsaw Rising of 1944* (Cambridge: Cambridge University Press, 1974), Joanna K. M. Hanson's *The Civilian Population and the Warsaw Upris-*

ing of 1944 (Cambridge: Cambridge University Press, 1982), Neil D. Orpen's *Airlift to Warsaw: The Rising of 1944* (Norman: University of Oklahoma Press, 1984), Michael Alfred Peszke's *Battle for Warsaw, 1939–1944* (Boulder: East European Monographs, 1995), and Andrew Borowiec's *Destroy Warsaw!: Hitler's Punishment, Stalin's Revenge* (Westport, Conn.: Praeger, 2001). Churchill's House of Commons speech about Britain's debt to the Poles is quoted in *The Formation of the Polish Community in Great Britain 1939–1950* by Keith Sword, with Norman Davies and Jan M. Ciechanowski (London: School of Slavonic and East European Studies, University of London, 1989), which is a useful study of the fate of the Poles in Britain after the war.

On the house under Calton Hill, see Graham Smith, "A Calotype View of Trinity College Church, Edinburgh, by David Octavius Hill and Robert Adamson," *Burlington Magazine* 126, no. 981 (December 1984): 781–82. My childhood clan directory was *The Scottish Tartans: With Historical Sketches of the Clans and Families* (Edinburgh: W. & A. K. Johnston, 1940). Background on the architect of my grandfather's Warsaw house is from Aldona Bartczakowa's *Franciszek Maria Lanci, 1799–1875* (Warsaw: Budownictwo i Architetektura, 1954). Biographical information on my paternal grandfather is contained in Władisław Czapliński's "Wspomnienie o Profesorze Rybczyńskim," *Tygodnik Powszechny,* no. 242 (undated). The reference to "happy unhappy lives" is from John Lukacs's *Confessions of an Original Sinner* (New York: Ticknor & Fields, 1990). I have quoted from Garry Wills's "Jesuits in Disarray," *New York Review of Books,* March 28, 2002, on Jesuit scholastics.

My discovery that Greek temples were intimately related to their surrounding landscape was made two years after Vincent Scully published his insightful *The Earth, the Temple and the Gods: Greek Sacred Architecture* (New Haven: Yale University Press, 1962), although I can't recall if I had already read his book at that time. I first described my sojourn in Formentera in *The Most Beautiful House in the World* and elaborated on the experience in "Formentera Spring," which was published in *House Beautiful,* November 1992, 14–20, and included in *Thoughts of Home: Reflections on Families, Houses, and Homelands from the Pages of* House Beautiful *Magazine,* Elaine Greene, ed. (New York: Hearst Books, 1995), 128–33.

The Mexican low-cost housing project is documented in Eric Dluhosch and Witold Rybczynski, "Sites, Services and Supports," *International Journal for Housing Science and Its Applications* 6, no. 1 (1982): 1–7. For a summary of Minimum Cost Housing Group projects, see "Seventeen Years of Minimum Cost Housing," Witold Rybczynski and Vikram Bhatt, eds., *Open House International* 13, no. 1 (1988): 1–82. Many of the people I met in the course of my travels in developing countries who were engaged in similar work were "outsiders": Alvaro Ortega; Krisno Nimpuno, who did interesting work on low-cost sanitation, was from Indonesia, had lived in Mozambique, and was based in Holland; Nick Wilkinson, who worked on flexible housing systems in Holland, edited *Open House* magazine at the University of Newcastle and later ended up in Cyprus; Tomasz Sudra was a Pole who taught at MIT, worked in Mexico, and finished his career with the United Nations in Kenya; John F. C. Turner, the British author of the classic *Freedom to Build,* championed self-help housing in Peru, Britain, and the United States; and Martin Pawley, well-known architectural writer and critic in England, worked on low-cost housing research in the United States and Peru in the 1970s. The story of "The Boathouse" has already been told in *The Most Beautiful House in the World* (New York: Penguin Books, 1989), and I have reused parts of that book here, though in altered form.

I write these essays under a serious impediment: I have a spotty memory. My British boyhood remains a collection of dim fragments, although my Canadian youth is in sharper focus. Photographs helped, especially as this narrative describes the making of an imaginative life that is in large part visual. Beginning in 1964, I kept travel journals, notebooks, and sketchbooks. The latter, in particular, were useful, since they are a record of what I was actually looking at. I have reproduced some prose fragments of that time here, not for their slim literary merit but because they throw light on my state of mind.

I would like to thank a number of people for their help in filling in the blanks. My mother patiently answered all my questions about events and people long gone. My father, who died in 1996, compiled copious diaries of his wartime experiences, and I want to thank my brother, Anthony, who collected this material into a biographical note. My uncle, Michał Hofman, now living in France, shared his boyhood memories of Mokotowska Street and the devastating events of 1944. Jurek Komorowski, whose grandfather and mine were best friends, generously spent time chatting about the past. Hugh Hartwell remembered jazz clubs and musicians of Montreal in the 1960s; my classmate Andrejs Skaburskis's recollections of being a student at McGill were a big help; and Bing Thom, a lifelong friend, reminded me of forgotten details of our time in Ottawa.

My wife, Shirley Hallam, indulged me in my reminiscences and cast her eye on the manuscript during its long gestation; and my agent, Andrew Wylie, provided vital support at a critical juncture. Thanks are due to my editor, Nan Graham, who was demanding when she had to be, and invariably helpful during various precarious moments during this unconventional—for me—undertaking. Susan M. S. Brown did a sterling copyediting job.

The Icehouse, Chestnut Hill
April 2002—June 2008

INDEX

NOTE: Bold page numbers refer to picture captions. WR refers to Witold Rybczynski, the author. WR Sr. refers to the author's father. Anna refers to Anna Hofman Rybczynski, the author's mother.